C-4901 CAREER EXAMINATION SERIES

This is your
PASSBOOK for...

Associate Safety & Health Inspector

Test Preparation Study Guide
Questions & Answers

COPYRIGHT NOTICE

This book is SOLELY intended for, is sold ONLY to, and its use is RESTRICTED to individual, bona fide applicants or candidates who qualify by virtue of having seriously filed applications for appropriate license, certificate, professional and/or promotional advancement, higher school matriculation, scholarship, or other legitimate requirements of education and/or governmental authorities.

This book is NOT intended for use, class instruction, tutoring, training, duplication, copying, reprinting, excerption, or adaptation, etc., by:

1) Other publishers
2) Proprietors and/or Instructors of "Coaching" and/or Preparatory Courses
3) Personnel and/or Training Divisions of commercial, industrial, and governmental organizations
4) Schools, colleges, or universities and/or their departments and staffs, including teachers and other personnel
5) Testing Agencies or Bureaus
6) Study groups which seek by the purchase of a single volume to copy and/or duplicate and/or adapt this material for use by the group as a whole without having purchased individual volumes for each of the members of the group
7) Et al.

Such persons would be in violation of appropriate Federal and State statutes.

PROVISION OF LICENSING AGREEMENTS – Recognized educational, commercial, industrial, and governmental institutions and organizations, and others legitimately engaged in educational pursuits, including training, testing, and measurement activities, may address request for a licensing agreement to the copyright owners, who will determine whether, and under what conditions, including fees and charges, the materials in this book may be used them. In other words, a licensing facility exists for the legitimate use of the material in this book on other than an individual basis. However, it is asseverated and affirmed here that the material in this book CANNOT be used without the receipt of the express permission of such a licensing agreement from the Publishers. Inquiries re licensing should be addressed to the company, attention rights and permissions department.

All rights reserved, including the right of reproduction in whole or in part, in any form or by any means, electronic or mechanical, including photocopying, recording, or by any information storage and retrieval system, without permission in writing from the Publisher.

Copyright © 2025 by
National Learning Corporation

212 Michael Drive, Syosset, NY 11791
(516) 921-8888 • www.passbooks.com
E-mail: info@passbooks.com

PASSBOOK® SERIES

THE *PASSBOOK® SERIES* has been created to prepare applicants and candidates for the ultimate academic battlefield – the examination room.

At some time in our lives, each and every one of us may be required to take an examination – for validation, matriculation, admission, qualification, registration, certification, or licensure.

Based on the assumption that every applicant or candidate has met the basic formal educational standards, has taken the required number of courses, and read the necessary texts, the *PASSBOOK® SERIES* furnishes the one special preparation which may assure passing with confidence, instead of failing with insecurity. Examination questions – together with answers – are furnished as the basic vehicle for study so that the mysteries of the examination and its compounding difficulties may be eliminated or diminished by a sure method.

This book is meant to help you pass your examination provided that you qualify and are serious in your objective.

The entire field is reviewed through the huge store of content information which is succinctly presented through a provocative and challenging approach – the question-and-answer method.

A climate of success is established by furnishing the correct answers at the end of each test.

You soon learn to recognize types of questions, forms of questions, and patterns of questioning. You may even begin to anticipate expected outcomes.

You perceive that many questions are repeated or adapted so that you can gain acute insights, which may enable you to score many sure points.

You learn how to confront new questions, or types of questions, and to attack them confidently and work out the correct answers.

You note objectives and emphases, and recognize pitfalls and dangers, so that you may make positive educational adjustments.

Moreover, you are kept fully informed in relation to new concepts, methods, practices, and directions in the field.

You discover that you are actually taking the examination all the time: you are preparing for the examination by "taking" an examination, not by reading extraneous and/or supererogatory textbooks.

In short, this PASSBOOK®, used directedly, should be an important factor in helping you to pass your test.

ASSOCIATE SAFETY AND HEALTH INSPECTOR

DUTIES:
As an Associate Safety and Health Inspector, you would perform and supervise staff performing inspections or consultations at public and private work sites and places of public assembly to ensure conformance with established occupational safety and health standards, identify unsafe conditions and work practices, and provide training to protect workers and the public. You would plan and schedule district office activities; supervise, train, and develop staff; review and monitor operations of the district office; provide training and education to employers; act as a safety and health resource for assigned program; and conduct the most difficult inspections or consultations.

SUBJECT OF EXAMINATION:
The written test is designed to test for knowledge, skills, and/or abilities in such areas as:
1. **Occupational health and safety including accident prevention and control** - These questions test for knowledge of the principles and practices of occupational health and safety, and accident prevention and control, including such areas as causes of accidents, accident rates, behavior and attitudes of workers and supervisors, accident investigations and interviewing techniques, and types of accident prevention and safety programs.
2. **Statutory and regulatory requirements relating to occupational health and safety, and building safety** - These questions are designed to test the candidates' knowledge of those State and Federal laws, rules and regulations that pertain to worker safety and health practices and building safety. Questions may be drawn from, but are not limited to, the Uniform Fire Prevention and Building Code, Occupational Health and Safety Administration, National Fire Protection Association, Life Safety Standards, and Department of Labor safety and health regulations.
3. **Preparing written material** - These questions test for the ability to present information clearly and accurately, and to organize paragraphs logically and comprehensibly. For some questions, you will be given information in two or three sentences followed by four restatements of the information. You must then choose the best version. For other questions, you will be given paragraphs with their sentences out of order. You must then choose, from four suggestions, the best order for the sentences.
4. **Supervision** - These questions test for knowledge of the principles and practices employed in planning, organizing, and controlling the activities of a work unit toward predetermined objectives. The concepts covered, usually in a situational question format, include such topics as assigning and reviewing work; evaluating performance; maintaining work standards; motivating and developing subordinates; implementing procedural change; increasing efficiency; and dealing with problems of absenteeism, morale, and discipline.
5. **Inspection and interviewing techniques** - These questions test your ability to select the proper course of action in situations which might occur during routine inspections. Question topics may cover, but will not be limited to, such areas as interviewing, gathering information and evidence, maintaining proper attitude, and handling irregularities and violations with integrity and sound judgment. Some questions may be in a situational format while others may deal with the proper principles and practices of inspection.
6. **Ensuring effective inter/intra agency communications** - These questions test for understanding of techniques for interacting effectively with individuals and agencies, to educate and inform them about topics of concern, to clarify agency programs or policies, to negotiate conflicts or resolve complaints, and to represent one's agency or program in a manner in keeping with good public relations practices. Questions may also cover interacting with the staff of one's own agency and/or that of other agencies in cooperative efforts of public outreach or service.

HOW TO TAKE A TEST

I. YOU MUST PASS AN EXAMINATION

A. WHAT EVERY CANDIDATE SHOULD KNOW

Examination applicants often ask us for help in preparing for the written test. What can I study in advance? What kinds of questions will be asked? How will the test be given? How will the papers be graded?

As an applicant for a civil service examination, you may be wondering about some of these things. Our purpose here is to suggest effective methods of advance study and to describe civil service examinations.

Your chances for success on this examination can be increased if you know how to prepare. Those "pre-examination jitters" can be reduced if you know what to expect. You can even experience an adventure in good citizenship if you know why civil service exams are given.

B. WHY ARE CIVIL SERVICE EXAMINATIONS GIVEN?

Civil service examinations are important to you in two ways. As a citizen, you want public jobs filled by employees who know how to do their work. As a job seeker, you want a fair chance to compete for that job on an equal footing with other candidates. The best-known means of accomplishing this two-fold goal is the competitive examination.

Exams are widely publicized throughout the nation. They may be administered for jobs in federal, state, city, municipal, town or village governments or agencies.

Any citizen may apply, with some limitations, such as the age or residence of applicants. Your experience and education may be reviewed to see whether you meet the requirements for the particular examination. When these requirements exist, they are reasonable and applied consistently to all applicants. Thus, a competitive examination may cause you some uneasiness now, but it is your privilege and safeguard.

C. HOW ARE CIVIL SERVICE EXAMS DEVELOPED?

Examinations are carefully written by trained technicians who are specialists in the field known as "psychological measurement," in consultation with recognized authorities in the field of work that the test will cover. These experts recommend the subject matter areas or skills to be tested; only those knowledges or skills important to your success on the job are included. The most reliable books and source materials available are used as references. Together, the experts and technicians judge the difficulty level of the questions.

Test technicians know how to phrase questions so that the problem is clearly stated. Their ethics do not permit "trick" or "catch" questions. Questions may have been tried out on sample groups, or subjected to statistical analysis, to determine their usefulness.

Written tests are often used in combination with performance tests, ratings of training and experience, and oral interviews. All of these measures combine to form the best-known means of finding the right person for the right job.

II. HOW TO PASS THE WRITTEN TEST

A. NATURE OF THE EXAMINATION

To prepare intelligently for civil service examinations, you should know how they differ from school examinations you have taken. In school you were assigned certain definite pages to read or subjects to cover. The examination questions were quite detailed and usually emphasized memory. Civil service exams, on the other hand, try to discover your present ability to perform the duties of a position, plus your potentiality to learn these duties. In other words, a civil service exam attempts to predict how successful you will be. Questions cover such a broad area that they cannot be as minute and detailed as school exam questions.

In the public service similar kinds of work, or positions, are grouped together in one "class." This process is known as *position-classification*. All the positions in a class are paid according to the salary range for that class. One class title covers all of these positions, and they are all tested by the same examination.

B. FOUR BASIC STEPS

1) Study the announcement

How, then, can you know what subjects to study? Our best answer is: "Learn as much as possible about the class of positions for which you've applied." The exam will test the knowledge, skills and abilities needed to do the work.

Your most valuable source of information about the position you want is the official exam announcement. This announcement lists the training and experience qualifications. Check these standards and apply only if you come reasonably close to meeting them.

The brief description of the position in the examination announcement offers some clues to the subjects which will be tested. Think about the job itself. Review the duties in your mind. Can you perform them, or are there some in which you are rusty? Fill in the blank spots in your preparation.

Many jurisdictions preview the written test in the exam announcement by including a section called "Knowledge and Abilities Required," "Scope of the Examination," or some similar heading. Here you will find out specifically what fields will be tested.

2) Review your own background

Once you learn in general what the position is all about, and what you need to know to do the work, ask yourself which subjects you already know fairly well and which need improvement. You may wonder whether to concentrate on improving your strong areas or on building some background in your fields of weakness. When the announcement has specified "some knowledge" or "considerable knowledge," or has used adjectives like "beginning principles of…" or "advanced … methods," you can get a clue as to the number and difficulty of questions to be asked in any given field. More questions, and hence broader coverage, would be included for those subjects which are more important in the work. Now weigh your strengths and weaknesses against the job requirements and prepare accordingly.

3) Determine the level of the position

Another way to tell how intensively you should prepare is to understand the level of the job for which you are applying. Is it the entering level? In other words, is this the position in which beginners in a field of work are hired? Or is it an intermediate or advanced level? Sometimes this is indicated by such words as "Junior" or "Senior" in the class title. Other jurisdictions use Roman numerals to designate the level – Clerk I, Clerk II, for example. The word "Supervisor" sometimes appears in the title. If the level is not indicated by the title, check the description of duties. Will you be working under very close supervision, or will you have responsibility for independent decisions in this work?

4) Choose appropriate study materials

Now that you know the subjects to be examined and the relative amount of each subject to be covered, you can choose suitable study materials. For beginning level jobs, or even advanced ones, if you have a pronounced weakness in some aspect of your training, read a modern, standard textbook in that field. Be sure it is up to date and has general coverage. Such books are normally available at your library, and the librarian will be glad to help you locate one. For entry-level positions, questions of appropriate difficulty are chosen – neither highly advanced questions, nor those too simple. Such questions require careful thought but not advanced training.

If the position for which you are applying is technical or advanced, you will read more advanced, specialized material. If you are already familiar with the basic principles of your field, elementary textbooks would waste your time. Concentrate on advanced textbooks and technical periodicals. Think through the concepts and review difficult problems in your field.

These are all general sources. You can get more ideas on your own initiative, following these leads. For example, training manuals and publications of the government agency which employs workers in your field can be useful, particularly for technical and professional positions. A letter or visit to the government department involved may result in more specific study suggestions, and certainly will provide you with a more definite idea of the exact nature of the position you are seeking.

III. KINDS OF TESTS

Tests are used for purposes other than measuring knowledge and ability to perform specified duties. For some positions, it is equally important to test ability to make adjustments to new situations or to profit from training. In others, basic mental abilities not dependent on information are essential. Questions which test these things may not appear as pertinent to the duties of the position as those which test for knowledge and information. Yet they are often highly important parts of a fair examination. For very general questions, it is almost impossible to help you direct your study efforts. What we can do is to point out some of the more common of these general abilities needed in public service positions and describe some typical questions.

1) General information

Broad, general information has been found useful for predicting job success in some kinds of work. This is tested in a variety of ways, from vocabulary lists to questions about current events. Basic background in some field of work, such as sociology or economics, may be sampled in a group of questions. Often these are principles which have become familiar to most persons through exposure rather than through formal training. It is difficult to advise you how to study for these questions; being alert to the world around you is our best suggestion.

2) Verbal ability

An example of an ability needed in many positions is verbal or language ability. Verbal ability is, in brief, the ability to use and understand words. Vocabulary and grammar tests are typical measures of this ability. Reading comprehension or paragraph interpretation questions are common in many kinds of civil service tests. You are given a paragraph of written material and asked to find its central meaning.

3) Numerical ability

Number skills can be tested by the familiar arithmetic problem, by checking paired lists of numbers to see which are alike and which are different, or by interpreting charts and graphs. In the latter test, a graph may be printed in the test booklet which you are asked to use as the basis for answering questions.

4) Observation

A popular test for law-enforcement positions is the observation test. A picture is shown to you for several minutes, then taken away. Questions about the picture test your ability to observe both details and larger elements.

5) Following directions

In many positions in the public service, the employee must be able to carry out written instructions dependably and accurately. You may be given a chart with several columns, each column listing a variety of information. The questions require you to carry out directions involving the information given in the chart.

6) Skills and aptitudes

Performance tests effectively measure some manual skills and aptitudes. When the skill is one in which you are trained, such as typing or shorthand, you can practice. These tests are often very much like those given in business school or high school courses. For many of the other skills and aptitudes, however, no short-time preparation can be made. Skills and abilities natural to you or that you have developed throughout your lifetime are being tested.

Many of the general questions just described provide all the data needed to answer the questions and ask you to use your reasoning ability to find the answers. Your best preparation for these tests, as well as for tests of facts and ideas, is to be at your physical and mental best. You, no doubt, have your own methods of getting into an exam-taking mood and keeping "in shape." The next section lists some ideas on this subject.

IV. KINDS OF QUESTIONS

Only rarely is the "essay" question, which you answer in narrative form, used in civil service tests. Civil service tests are usually of the short-answer type. Full instructions for answering these questions will be given to you at the examination. But in case this is your first experience with short-answer questions and separate answer sheets, here is what you need to know:

1) **Multiple-choice Questions**

Most popular of the short-answer questions is the "multiple choice" or "best answer" question. It can be used, for example, to test for factual knowledge, ability to solve problems or judgment in meeting situations found at work.

A multiple-choice question is normally one of three types—
- It can begin with an incomplete statement followed by several possible endings. You are to find the one ending which *best* completes the statement, although some of the others may not be entirely wrong.
- It can also be a complete statement in the form of a question which is answered by choosing one of the statements listed.

- It can be in the form of a problem – again you select the best answer.

Here is an example of a multiple-choice question with a discussion which should give you some clues as to the method for choosing the right answer:

When an employee has a complaint about his assignment, the action which will *best* help him overcome his difficulty is to
- A. discuss his difficulty with his coworkers
- B. take the problem to the head of the organization
- C. take the problem to the person who gave him the assignment
- D. say nothing to anyone about his complaint

In answering this question, you should study each of the choices to find which is best. Consider choice "A" – Certainly an employee may discuss his complaint with fellow employees, but no change or improvement can result, and the complaint remains unresolved. Choice "B" is a poor choice since the head of the organization probably does not know what assignment you have been given, and taking your problem to him is known as "going over the head" of the supervisor. The supervisor, or person who made the assignment, is the person who can clarify it or correct any injustice. Choice "C" is, therefore, correct. To say nothing, as in choice "D," is unwise. Supervisors have and interest in knowing the problems employees are facing, and the employee is seeking a solution to his problem.

2) True/False Questions

The "true/false" or "right/wrong" form of question is sometimes used. Here a complete statement is given. Your job is to decide whether the statement is right or wrong.

SAMPLE: A roaming cell-phone call to a nearby city costs less than a non-roaming call to a distant city.

This statement is wrong, or false, since roaming calls are more expensive.

This is not a complete list of all possible question forms, although most of the others are variations of these common types. You will always get complete directions for answering questions. Be sure you understand *how* to mark your answers – ask questions until you do.

V. RECORDING YOUR ANSWERS

Computer terminals are used more and more today for many different kinds of exams.

For an examination with very few applicants, you may be told to record your answers in the test booklet itself. Separate answer sheets are much more common. If this separate answer sheet is to be scored by machine – and this is often the case – it is highly important that you mark your answers correctly in order to get credit.

An electronic scoring machine is often used in civil service offices because of the speed with which papers can be scored. Machine-scored answer sheets must be marked with a pencil, which will be given to you. This pencil has a high graphite content which responds to the electronic scoring machine. As a matter of fact, stray dots may register as answers, so do not let your pencil rest on the answer sheet while you are pondering the correct answer. Also, if your pencil lead breaks or is otherwise defective, ask for another.

Since the answer sheet will be dropped in a slot in the scoring machine, be careful not to bend the corners or get the paper crumpled.

The answer sheet normally has five vertical columns of numbers, with 30 numbers to a column. These numbers correspond to the question numbers in your test booklet. After each number, going across the page are four or five pairs of dotted lines. These short dotted lines have small letters or numbers above them. The first two pairs may also have a "T" or "F" above the letters. This indicates that the first two pairs only are to be used if the questions are of the true-false type. If the questions are multiple choice, disregard the "T" and "F" and pay attention only to the small letters or numbers.

Answer your questions in the manner of the sample that follows:

32. The largest city in the United States is
    A. Washington, D.C.
    B. New York City
    C. Chicago
    D. Detroit
    E. San Francisco

1) Choose the answer you think is best. (New York City is the largest, so "B" is correct.)
2) Find the row of dotted lines numbered the same as the question you are answering. (Find row number 32)
3) Find the pair of dotted lines corresponding to the answer. (Find the pair of lines under the mark "B.")
4) Make a solid black mark between the dotted lines.

VI. BEFORE THE TEST

Common sense will help you find procedures to follow to get ready for an examination. Too many of us, however, overlook these sensible measures. Indeed, nervousness and fatigue have been found to be the most serious reasons why applicants fail to do their best on civil service tests. Here is a list of reminders:

- Begin your preparation early – Don't wait until the last minute to go scurrying around for books and materials or to find out what the position is all about.
- Prepare continuously – An hour a night for a week is better than an all-night cram session. This has been definitely established. What is more, a night a week for a month will return better dividends than crowding your study into a shorter period of time.
- Locate the place of the exam – You have been sent a notice telling you when and where to report for the examination. If the location is in a different town or otherwise unfamiliar to you, it would be well to inquire the best route and learn something about the building.
- Relax the night before the test – Allow your mind to rest. Do not study at all that night. Plan some mild recreation or diversion; then go to bed early and get a good night's sleep.
- Get up early enough to make a leisurely trip to the place for the test – This way unforeseen events, traffic snarls, unfamiliar buildings, etc. will not upset you.
- Dress comfortably – A written test is not a fashion show. You will be known by number and not by name, so wear something comfortable.

- Leave excess paraphernalia at home – Shopping bags and odd bundles will get in your way. You need bring only the items mentioned in the official notice you received; usually everything you need is provided. Do not bring reference books to the exam. They will only confuse those last minutes and be taken away from you when in the test room.
- Arrive somewhat ahead of time – If because of transportation schedules you must get there very early, bring a newspaper or magazine to take your mind off yourself while waiting.
- Locate the examination room – When you have found the proper room, you will be directed to the seat or part of the room where you will sit. Sometimes you are given a sheet of instructions to read while you are waiting. Do not fill out any forms until you are told to do so; just read them and be prepared.
- Relax and prepare to listen to the instructions
- If you have any physical problem that may keep you from doing your best, be sure to tell the test administrator. If you are sick or in poor health, you really cannot do your best on the exam. You can come back and take the test some other time.

VII. AT THE TEST

The day of the test is here and you have the test booklet in your hand. The temptation to get going is very strong. Caution! There is more to success than knowing the right answers. You must know how to identify your papers and understand variations in the type of short-answer question used in this particular examination. Follow these suggestions for maximum results from your efforts:

1) Cooperate with the monitor

The test administrator has a duty to create a situation in which you can be as much at ease as possible. He will give instructions, tell you when to begin, check to see that you are marking your answer sheet correctly, and so on. He is not there to guard you, although he will see that your competitors do not take unfair advantage. He wants to help you do your best.

2) Listen to all instructions

Don't jump the gun! Wait until you understand all directions. In most civil service tests you get more time than you need to answer the questions. So don't be in a hurry. Read each word of instructions until you clearly understand the meaning. Study the examples, listen to all announcements and follow directions. Ask questions if you do not understand what to do.

3) Identify your papers

Civil service exams are usually identified by number only. You will be assigned a number; you must not put your name on your test papers. Be sure to copy your number correctly. Since more than one exam may be given, copy your exact examination title.

4) Plan your time

Unless you are told that a test is a "speed" or "rate of work" test, speed itself is usually not important. Time enough to answer all the questions will be provided, but this does not mean that you have all day. An overall time limit has been set. Divide the total time (in minutes) by the number of questions to determine the approximate time you have for each question.

5) Do not linger over difficult questions

If you come across a difficult question, mark it with a paper clip (useful to have along) and come back to it when you have been through the booklet. One caution if you do this – be sure to skip a number on your answer sheet as well. Check often to be sure that you have not lost your place and that you are marking in the row numbered the same as the question you are answering.

6) Read the questions

Be sure you know what the question asks! Many capable people are unsuccessful because they failed to *read* the questions correctly.

7) Answer all questions

Unless you have been instructed that a penalty will be deducted for incorrect answers, it is better to guess than to omit a question.

8) Speed tests

It is often better NOT to guess on speed tests. It has been found that on timed tests people are tempted to spend the last few seconds before time is called in marking answers at random – without even reading them – in the hope of picking up a few extra points. To discourage this practice, the instructions may warn you that your score will be "corrected" for guessing. That is, a penalty will be applied. The incorrect answers will be deducted from the correct ones, or some other penalty formula will be used.

9) Review your answers

If you finish before time is called, go back to the questions you guessed or omitted to give them further thought. Review other answers if you have time.

10) Return your test materials

If you are ready to leave before others have finished or time is called, take ALL your materials to the monitor and leave quietly. Never take any test material with you. The monitor can discover whose papers are not complete, and taking a test booklet may be grounds for disqualification.

VIII. EXAMINATION TECHNIQUES

1) Read the general instructions carefully. These are usually printed on the first page of the exam booklet. As a rule, these instructions refer to the timing of the examination; the fact that you should not start work until the signal and must stop work at a signal, etc. If there are any *special* instructions, such as a choice of questions to be answered, make sure that you note this instruction carefully.

2) When you are ready to start work on the examination, that is as soon as the signal has been given, read the instructions to each question booklet, underline any key words or phrases, such as *least, best, outline, describe* and the like. In this way you will tend to answer as requested rather than discover on reviewing your paper that you *listed without describing*, that you selected the *worst* choice rather than the *best* choice, etc.

3) If the examination is of the objective or multiple-choice type – that is, each question will also give a series of possible answers: A, B, C or D, and you are called upon to select the best answer and write the letter next to that answer on your answer paper – it is advisable to start answering each question in turn. There may be anywhere from 50 to 100 such questions in the three or four hours allotted and you can see how much time would be taken if you read through all the questions before beginning to answer any. Furthermore, if you come across a question or group of questions which you know would be difficult to answer, it would undoubtedly affect your handling of all the other questions.

4) If the examination is of the essay type and contains but a few questions, it is a moot point as to whether you should read all the questions before starting to answer any one. Of course, if you are given a choice – say five out of seven and the like – then it is essential to read all the questions so you can eliminate the two that are most difficult. If, however, you are asked to answer all the questions, there may be danger in trying to answer the easiest one first because you may find that you will spend too much time on it. The best technique is to answer the first question, then proceed to the second, etc.

5) Time your answers. Before the exam begins, write down the time it started, then add the time allowed for the examination and write down the time it must be completed, then divide the time available somewhat as follows:
    - If 3-1/2 hours are allowed, that would be 210 minutes. If you have 80 objective-type questions, that would be an average of 2-1/2 minutes per question. Allow yourself no more than 2 minutes per question, or a total of 160 minutes, which will permit about 50 minutes to review.
    - If for the time allotment of 210 minutes there are 7 essay questions to answer, that would average about 30 minutes a question. Give yourself only 25 minutes per question so that you have about 35 minutes to review.

6) The most important instruction is to *read each question* and make sure you know what is wanted. The second most important instruction is to *time yourself properly* so that you answer every question. The third most important instruction is to *answer every question*. Guess if you have to but include something for each question. Remember that you will receive no credit for a blank and will probably receive some credit if you write something in answer to an essay question. If you guess a letter – say "B" for a multiple-choice question – you may have guessed right. If you leave a blank as an answer to a multiple-choice question, the examiners may respect your feelings but it will not add a point to your score. Some exams may penalize you for wrong answers, so in such cases *only*, you may not want to guess unless you have some basis for your answer.

7) Suggestions
    a. Objective-type questions
        1. Examine the question booklet for proper sequence of pages and questions
        2. Read all instructions carefully
        3. Skip any question which seems too difficult; return to it after all other questions have been answered
        4. Apportion your time properly; do not spend too much time on any single question or group of questions

5. Note and underline key words – *all, most, fewest, least, best, worst, same, opposite,* etc.
6. Pay particular attention to negatives
7. Note unusual option, e.g., unduly long, short, complex, different or similar in content to the body of the question
8. Observe the use of "hedging" words – *probably, may, most likely,* etc.
9. Make sure that your answer is put next to the same number as the question
10. Do not second-guess unless you have good reason to believe the second answer is definitely more correct
11. Cross out original answer if you decide another answer is more accurate; do not erase until you are ready to hand your paper in
12. Answer all questions; guess unless instructed otherwise
13. Leave time for review

  b. Essay questions
    1. Read each question carefully
    2. Determine exactly what is wanted. Underline key words or phrases.
    3. Decide on outline or paragraph answer
    4. Include many different points and elements unless asked to develop any one or two points or elements
    5. Show impartiality by giving pros and cons unless directed to select one side only
    6. Make and write down any assumptions you find necessary to answer the questions
    7. Watch your English, grammar, punctuation and choice of words
    8. Time your answers; don't crowd material

8) Answering the essay question

Most essay questions can be answered by framing the specific response around several key words or ideas. Here are a few such key words or ideas:

M's: manpower, materials, methods, money, management
P's: purpose, program, policy, plan, procedure, practice, problems, pitfalls, personnel, public relations

  a. Six basic steps in handling problems:
    1. Preliminary plan and background development
    2. Collect information, data and facts
    3. Analyze and interpret information, data and facts
    4. Analyze and develop solutions as well as make recommendations
    5. Prepare report and sell recommendations
    6. Install recommendations and follow up effectiveness

  b. Pitfalls to avoid
    1. *Taking things for granted* – A statement of the situation does not necessarily imply that each of the elements is necessarily true; for example, a complaint may be invalid and biased so that all that can be taken for granted is that a complaint has been registered

2. *Considering only one side of a situation* – Wherever possible, indicate several alternatives and then point out the reasons you selected the best one
3. *Failing to indicate follow up* – Whenever your answer indicates action on your part, make certain that you will take proper follow-up action to see how successful your recommendations, procedures or actions turn out to be
4. *Taking too long in answering any single question* – Remember to time your answers properly

IX. AFTER THE TEST

Scoring procedures differ in detail among civil service jurisdictions although the general principles are the same. Whether the papers are hand-scored or graded by machine we have described, they are nearly always graded by number. That is, the person who marks the paper knows only the number – never the name – of the applicant. Not until all the papers have been graded will they be matched with names. If other tests, such as training and experience or oral interview ratings have been given, scores will be combined. Different parts of the examination usually have different weights. For example, the written test might count 60 percent of the final grade, and a rating of training and experience 40 percent. In many jurisdictions, veterans will have a certain number of points added to their grades.

After the final grade has been determined, the names are placed in grade order and an eligible list is established. There are various methods for resolving ties between those who get the same final grade – probably the most common is to place first the name of the person whose application was received first. Job offers are made from the eligible list in the order the names appear on it. You will be notified of your grade and your rank as soon as all these computations have been made. This will be done as rapidly as possible.

People who are found to meet the requirements in the announcement are called "eligibles." Their names are put on a list of eligible candidates. An eligible's chances of getting a job depend on how high he stands on this list and how fast agencies are filling jobs from the list.

When a job is to be filled from a list of eligibles, the agency asks for the names of people on the list of eligibles for that job. When the civil service commission receives this request, it sends to the agency the names of the three people highest on this list. Or, if the job to be filled has specialized requirements, the office sends the agency the names of the top three persons who meet these requirements from the general list.

The appointing officer makes a choice from among the three people whose names were sent to him. If the selected person accepts the appointment, the names of the others are put back on the list to be considered for future openings.

That is the rule in hiring from all kinds of eligible lists, whether they are for typist, carpenter, chemist, or something else. For every vacancy, the appointing officer has his choice of any one of the top three eligibles on the list. This explains why the person whose name is on top of the list sometimes does not get an appointment when some of the persons lower on the list do. If the appointing officer chooses the second or third eligible, the No. 1 eligible does not get a job at once, but stays on the list until he is appointed or the list is terminated.

X. HOW TO PASS THE INTERVIEW TEST

The examination for which you applied requires an oral interview test. You have already taken the written test and you are now being called for the interview test – the final part of the formal examination.

You may think that it is not possible to prepare for an interview test and that there are no procedures to follow during an interview. Our purpose is to point out some things you can do in advance that will help you and some good rules to follow and pitfalls to avoid while you are being interviewed.

What is an interview supposed to test?

The written examination is designed to test the technical knowledge and competence of the candidate; the oral is designed to evaluate intangible qualities, not readily measured otherwise, and to establish a list showing the relative fitness of each candidate – as measured against his competitors – for the position sought. Scoring is not on the basis of "right" and "wrong," but on a sliding scale of values ranging from "not passable" to "outstanding." As a matter of fact, it is possible to achieve a relatively low score without a single "incorrect" answer because of evident weakness in the qualities being measured.

Occasionally, an examination may consist entirely of an oral test – either an individual or a group oral. In such cases, information is sought concerning the technical knowledges and abilities of the candidate, since there has been no written examination for this purpose. More commonly, however, an oral test is used to supplement a written examination.

Who conducts interviews?

The composition of oral boards varies among different jurisdictions. In nearly all, a representative of the personnel department serves as chairman. One of the members of the board may be a representative of the department in which the candidate would work. In some cases, "outside experts" are used, and, frequently, a businessman or some other representative of the general public is asked to serve. Labor and management or other special groups may be represented. The aim is to secure the services of experts in the appropriate field.

However the board is composed, it is a good idea (and not at all improper or unethical) to ascertain in advance of the interview who the members are and what groups they represent. When you are introduced to them, you will have some idea of their backgrounds and interests, and at least you will not stutter and stammer over their names.

What should be done before the interview?

While knowledge about the board members is useful and takes some of the surprise element out of the interview, there is other preparation which is more substantive. It *is* possible to prepare for an oral interview – in several ways:

1) Keep a copy of your application and review it carefully before the interview

This may be the only document before the oral board, and the starting point of the interview. Know what education and experience you have listed there, and the sequence and dates of all of it. Sometimes the board will ask you to review the highlights of your experience for them; you should not have to hem and haw doing it.

2) Study the class specification and the examination announcement

Usually, the oral board has one or both of these to guide them. The qualities, characteristics or knowledges required by the position sought are stated in these documents. They offer valuable clues as to the nature of the oral interview. For example, if the job involves supervisory responsibilities, the announcement will usually indicate that knowledge of modern supervisory methods and the qualifications of the candidate as a supervisor will be tested. If so, you can expect such questions, frequently in the form of a hypothetical situation which you are expected to solve. NEVER go into an oral without knowledge of the duties and responsibilities of the job you seek.

3) Think through each qualification required

Try to visualize the kind of questions you would ask if you were a board member. How well could you answer them? Try especially to appraise your own knowledge and background in each area, *measured against the job sought*, and identify any areas in which you are weak. Be critical and realistic – do not flatter yourself.

4) Do some general reading in areas in which you feel you may be weak

For example, if the job involves supervision and your past experience has NOT, some general reading in supervisory methods and practices, particularly in the field of human relations, might be useful. Do NOT study agency procedures or detailed manuals. The oral board will be testing your understanding and capacity, not your memory.

5) Get a good night's sleep and watch your general health and mental attitude

You will want a clear head at the interview. Take care of a cold or any other minor ailment, and of course, no hangovers.

What should be done on the day of the interview?

Now comes the day of the interview itself. Give yourself plenty of time to get there. Plan to arrive somewhat ahead of the scheduled time, particularly if your appointment is in the fore part of the day. If a previous candidate fails to appear, the board might be ready for you a bit early. By early afternoon an oral board is almost invariably behind schedule if there are many candidates, and you may have to wait. Take along a book or magazine to read, or your application to review, but leave any extraneous material in the waiting room when you go in for your interview. In any event, relax and compose yourself.

The matter of dress is important. The board is forming impressions about you – from your experience, your manners, your attitude, and your appearance. Give your personal appearance careful attention. Dress your best, but not your flashiest. Choose conservative, appropriate clothing, and be sure it is immaculate. This is a business interview, and your appearance should indicate that you regard it as such. Besides, being well groomed and properly dressed will help boost your confidence.

Sooner or later, someone will call your name and escort you into the interview room. *This is it.* From here on you are on your own. It is too late for any more preparation. But remember, you asked for this opportunity to prove your fitness, and you are here because your request was granted.

What happens when you go in?

The usual sequence of events will be as follows: The clerk (who is often the board stenographer) will introduce you to the chairman of the oral board, who will introduce you to the other members of the board. Acknowledge the introductions before you sit down. Do not be surprised if you find a microphone facing you or a stenotypist sitting by. Oral interviews are usually recorded in the event of an appeal or other review.

Usually the chairman of the board will open the interview by reviewing the highlights of your education and work experience from your application – primarily for the benefit of the other members of the board, as well as to get the material into the record. Do not interrupt or comment unless there is an error or significant misinterpretation; if that is the case, do not hesitate. But do not quibble about insignificant matters. Also, he will usually ask you some question about your education, experience or your present job – partly to get you to start talking and to establish the interviewing "rapport." He may start the actual questioning, or turn it over to one of the other members. Frequently, each member undertakes the questioning on a particular area, one in which he is perhaps most competent, so you can expect each member to participate in the examination. Because time is limited, you may also expect some rather abrupt switches in the direction the questioning takes, so do not be upset by it. Normally, a board member will not pursue a single line of questioning unless he discovers a particular strength or weakness.

After each member has participated, the chairman will usually ask whether any member has any further questions, then will ask you if you have anything you wish to add. Unless you are expecting this question, it may floor you. Worse, it may start you off on an extended, extemporaneous speech. The board is not usually seeking more information. The question is principally to offer you a last opportunity to present further qualifications or to indicate that you have nothing to add. So, if you feel that a significant qualification or characteristic has been overlooked, it is proper to point it out in a sentence or so. Do not compliment the board on the thoroughness of their examination – they have been sketchy, and you know it. If you wish, merely say, "No thank you, I have nothing further to add." This is a point where you can "talk yourself out" of a good impression or fail to present an important bit of information. Remember, *you close the interview yourself.*

The chairman will then say, "That is all, Mr. _____, thank you." Do not be startled; the interview is over, and quicker than you think. Thank him, gather your belongings and take your leave. Save your sigh of relief for the other side of the door.

How to put your best foot forward

Throughout this entire process, you may feel that the board individually and collectively is trying to pierce your defenses, seek out your hidden weaknesses and embarrass and confuse you. Actually, this is not true. They are obliged to make an appraisal of your qualifications for the job you are seeking, and they want to see you in your best light. Remember, they must interview all candidates and a non-cooperative candidate may become a failure in spite of their best efforts to bring out his qualifications. Here are 15 suggestions that will help you:

1) Be natural – Keep your attitude confident, not cocky

If you are not confident that you can do the job, do not expect the board to be. Do not apologize for your weaknesses, try to bring out your strong points. The board is interested in a positive, not negative, presentation. Cockiness will antagonize any board member and make him wonder if you are covering up a weakness by a false show of strength.

2) Get comfortable, but don't lounge or sprawl

Sit erectly but not stiffly. A careless posture may lead the board to conclude that you are careless in other things, or at least that you are not impressed by the importance of the occasion. Either conclusion is natural, even if incorrect. Do not fuss with your clothing, a pencil or an ashtray. Your hands may occasionally be useful to emphasize a point; do not let them become a point of distraction.

3) Do not wisecrack or make small talk

This is a serious situation, and your attitude should show that you consider it as such. Further, the time of the board is limited – they do not want to waste it, and neither should you.

4) Do not exaggerate your experience or abilities

In the first place, from information in the application or other interviews and sources, the board may know more about you than you think. Secondly, you probably will not get away with it. An experienced board is rather adept at spotting such a situation, so do not take the chance.

5) If you know a board member, do not make a point of it, yet do not hide it

Certainly you are not fooling him, and probably not the other members of the board. Do not try to take advantage of your acquaintanceship – it will probably do you little good.

6) Do not dominate the interview

Let the board do that. They will give you the clues – do not assume that you have to do all the talking. Realize that the board has a number of questions to ask you, and do not try to take up all the interview time by showing off your extensive knowledge of the answer to the first one.

7) Be attentive

You only have 20 minutes or so, and you should keep your attention at its sharpest throughout. When a member is addressing a problem or question to you, give him your undivided attention. Address your reply principally to him, but do not exclude the other board members.

8) Do not interrupt

A board member may be stating a problem for you to analyze. He will ask you a question when the time comes. Let him state the problem, and wait for the question.

9) Make sure you understand the question

Do not try to answer until you are sure what the question is. If it is not clear, restate it in your own words or ask the board member to clarify it for you. However, do not haggle about minor elements.

10) Reply promptly but not hastily

A common entry on oral board rating sheets is "candidate responded readily," or "candidate hesitated in replies." Respond as promptly and quickly as you can, but do not jump to a hasty, ill-considered answer.

11) Do not be peremptory in your answers

A brief answer is proper – but do not fire your answer back. That is a losing game from your point of view. The board member can probably ask questions much faster than you can answer them.

12) Do not try to create the answer you think the board member wants

He is interested in what kind of mind you have and how it works – not in playing games. Furthermore, he can usually spot this practice and will actually grade you down on it.

13) Do not switch sides in your reply merely to agree with a board member

Frequently, a member will take a contrary position merely to draw you out and to see if you are willing and able to defend your point of view. Do not start a debate, yet do not surrender a good position. If a position is worth taking, it is worth defending.

14) Do not be afraid to admit an error in judgment if you are shown to be wrong

The board knows that you are forced to reply without any opportunity for careful consideration. Your answer may be demonstrably wrong. If so, admit it and get on with the interview.

15) Do not dwell at length on your present job

The opening question may relate to your present assignment. Answer the question but do not go into an extended discussion. You are being examined for a *new* job, not your present one. As a matter of fact, try to phrase ALL your answers in terms of the job for which you are being examined.

Basis of Rating

Probably you will forget most of these "do's" and "don'ts" when you walk into the oral interview room. Even remembering them all will not ensure you a passing grade. Perhaps you did not have the qualifications in the first place. But remembering them will help you to put your best foot forward, without treading on the toes of the board members.

Rumor and popular opinion to the contrary notwithstanding, an oral board wants you to make the best appearance possible. They know you are under pressure – but they also want to see how you respond to it as a guide to what your reaction would be under the pressures of the job you seek. They will be influenced by the degree of poise you display, the personal traits you show and the manner in which you respond.

ABOUT THIS BOOK

This book contains tests divided into Examination Sections. Go through each test, answering every question in the margin. We have also attached a sample answer sheet at the back of the book that can be removed and used. At the end of each test look at the answer key and check your answers. On the ones you got wrong, look at the right answer choice and learn. Do not fill in the answers first. Do not memorize the questions and answers, but understand the answer and principles involved. On your test, the questions will likely be different from the samples. Questions are changed and new ones added. If you understand these past questions you should have success with any changes that arise. Tests may consist of several types of questions. We have additional books on each subject should more study be advisable or necessary for you. Finally, the more you study, the better prepared you will be. This book is intended to be the last thing you study before you walk into the examination room. Prior study of relevant texts is also recommended. NLC publishes some of these in our Fundamental Series. Knowledge and good sense are important factors in passing your exam. Good luck also helps. So now study this Passbook, absorb the material contained within and take that knowledge into the examination. Then do your best to pass that exam.

EXAMINATION SECTION

SAFETY
EXAMINATION SECTION
TEST 1

DIRECTIONS: Each question or incomplete statement is followed by several suggested answers or completions. Select the one that BEST answers the question or completes the statement. *PRINT THE LETTER OF THE CORRECT ANSWER IN THE SPACE AT THE RIGHT.*

1. Which one of the following is an INCORRECT safety guideline? 1.____

    A. All working conditions and equipment should be considered carefully before beginning an operation.
    B. Aisles should be lighted properly.
    C. Personnel should be provided with protective clothing essential to safe performance of a task.
    D. In manual lifting, the worker must keep his knees straight and lift with the arm muscles.

2. Of the following, the supply item with the GREATEST susceptibility to spontaneous heating is 2.____

    A. alcohol, ethyl   B. kerosene
    C. candles   D. turpentine

Questions 3-7.

DIRECTIONS: Questions 3 through 7 are descriptions of accidents that occurred in a warehouse. For each accident, choose the letter in front of the safety measure that is MOST likely to prevent a repetition of the accident indicated.

<u>SAFETY MEASURE</u>

   A. Posting warning signs
   B. Redesign of layout or facilities
   C. Repairing, improving or replacing supplies, tools or equipment
   D. Training the staff in safe practices

3. After a new all-glass door was installed at the entrance to the warehouse, one of the employees banged his head into the door causing a large lump on his forehead when he failed to realize that the door was closed. 3.____

4. While tieing up a package with manila rope, an employee got several small rope splinters in his right hand and he had to have medical treatment to remove the splinters. 4.____

5. An employee discovered a small fire in a wastepaper basket but was unable to prevent it from spreading because all the nearby fire extinguishers were inaccessible due to skids of material being stacked in front of the extinguishers. 5.____

6. When a laborer attempted to drop the tailgate of a delivery truck while the truck was being backed into the loading dock, he had his fingers crushed when the truck continued to move while he was working on lowering the tailgate. 6.____

1

7. An employee carrying a carton with both hands tripped over a broom which had been left lying in an aisle by another employee after the latter had swept the aisle.   7._____

8. Safety experts agree that accidents can probably BEST be prevented by   8._____

   A. developing safety consciousness among employees
   B. developing a program which publicizes major accidents
   C. penalizing employees the first time they do not follow safety procedures
   D. giving recognition to employees with accident-free records

9. The accident records of many agencies indicate that most on-the-job injuries are caused by the unsafe acts of their employees.
   Which one of the following statements pinpoints the MOST probable cause of this safety problem?   9._____

   A. Responsibility for preventing on-the-job accidents has not been delegated.
   B. Lack of proper supervision has permitted these unsafe actions to continue.
   C. No consideration has been given to eliminating environmental job hazards.
   D. Penalties for causing on-the-job accidents are not sufficiently severe.

10. Which of the following methods is LEAST essential to the success of an accident prevention program?   10._____

    A. Determining corrective measures by analyzing the causes of accidents and making recommendations to eliminate them
    B. Educating employees as to the importance of safe working conditions and methods
    C. Determining accident causes by seeking out the conditions from which each accident has developed
    D. Holding each supervisor responsible for accidents occurring during the on-the-job performance of his immediate subordinates

11. The effectiveness of a public relations program in a public agency is BEST indicated by the   11._____

    A. amount of mass media publicity favorable to the policies of the agency
    B. morale of those employees who directly serve the patrons of the agency
    C. public's understanding and support of the agency's program and policies
    D. number of complaints received by the agency from patrons using its facilities

12. Buttered bread and coffee dropped on an office floor in a terminal are   12._____

    A. minor hazards which should cause no serious injury
    B. unattractive, but not dangerous
    C. the most dangerous types of office hazards
    D. hazards which should be corrected immediately

13. A laborer was sent upstairs to get a 20-pound sack of rock salt. While going downstairs and reading the printing on the sack, he fell, and the sack of rock salt fell and broke his toe.
    Which of the following is MOST likely to have been the MOST important cause of the accident?
    The   13._____

A. stairs were beginning to become worn
B. laborer was carrying too heavy a sack of rock salt
C. rock salt was in a place that was too inaccessible
D. laborer was not careful about the way he went down the stairs

14. A COMMONLY recommended safe distance between the foot of an extension ladder and the wall against which it is placed is

A. 3 feet for ladders less than 18 feet in height
B. between 3 feet and 6 feet for ladders less than 18 feet in length
C. 1/8 the length of the extended ladder
D. 1/4 the length of the extended ladder

15. The BEST type of fire extinguisher for electrical fires is the _____ extinguisher.

A. dry chemical   B. foam
C. carbon monoxide   D. baking soda-acid

16. A Class A extinguisher should be used for fires in

A. potassium, magnesium, zinc, sodium
B. electrical wiring
C. oil, gasoline
D. wood, paper, and textiles

17. The one of the following which is NOT a safe practice when lifting heavy objects is:

A. Keep the back as nearly upright as possible
B. If the object feels too heavy, keep lifting until you get help
C. Spread the feet apart
D. Use the arm and leg muscles

18. In a shop, it would be MOST necessary to provide a fitted cover on the metal container for

A. old paint brushes   B. oily rags and waste
C. sand   D. broken glass

19. Safety shoes usually have the unique feature of

A. extra hard heels and soles to prevent nails from piercing the shoes
B. special leather to prevent the piercing of the shoes by falling objects
C. a metal guard over the toes which is built into the shoes
D. a non-slip tread on the heels and soles

20. Of the following, the MOST important factor contributing to a helper's safety on the job is for him to

A. work slowly   B. wear gloves
C. be alert   D. know his job well

21. If it is necessary for you to lift one end of a piece of heavy equipment with a crowbar in order to allow a maintainer to work underneath it, the BEST of the following procedures to follow is to

    A. support the handle of the bar on a box
    B. insert temporary blocks to support the piece
    C. call the supervisor to help you
    D. wear heavy gloves

21.____

22. Of the following, the MOST important reason for not letting oily rags accumulate in an open storage bin is that they

    A. may start a fire by spontaneous combustion
    B. will drip oil onto other items in the bin
    C. may cause a foul odor
    D. will make the area messy

22.____

23. Of the following, the BEST method to employ in putting out a gasoline fire is to

    A. use a bucket of water
    B. smother it with rags
    C. use a carbon dioxide extinguisher
    D. use a carbon tetrachloride extinguisher

23.____

24. When opening an emergency exit door set in the sidewalk, the door should be raised slowly to avoid

    A. a sudden rush of air from the street
    B. making unnecessary noise
    C. damage to the sidewalk
    D. injuring pedestrians

24.____

25. The BEST reason to turn off lights when cleaning lampshades on electrical fixtures is to

    A. conserve energy
    B. avoid electrical shock
    C. prevent breakage of lightbulbs
    D. prevent unnecessary eye strain

25.____

KEY (CORRECT ANSWERS)

1. D
2. D
3. A
4. D
5. B

6. D
7. D
8. A
9. B
10. D

11. C
12. D
13. D
14. D
15. A

16. D
17. B
18. B
19. C
20. C

21. B
22. A
23. C
24. D
25. B

TEST 2

DIRECTIONS: Each question or incomplete statement is followed by several suggested answers or completions. Select the one that BEST answers the question or completes the statement. *PRINT THE LETTER OF THE CORRECT ANSWER IN THE SPACE AT THE RIGHT.*

1. The MOST important reason for roping off a work area in a terminal is to

   A. protect the public
   B. protect the repair crew
   C. prevent distraction of the crew by the public
   D. prevent delays to the public

   1.____

2. Shoes which have a sponge rubber sole should NOT be worn around a work area because such a sole

   A. will wear quickly
   B. is not waterproof
   C. does not keep the feet warm
   D. is easily punctured by steel objects

   2.____

3. When repair work is being done on an elevated structure, canvas spreads are suspended under the working area MAINLY to

   A. reduce noise
   B. discourage crowds
   C. protect the structure
   D. protect pedestrians

   3.____

4. It is poor practice to hold a piece of wood in the hands or lap when tightening a screw in the wood.
   This is for the reason that

   A. sufficient leverage cannot be obtained
   B. the screwdriver may bend
   C. the wood will probably split
   D. personal injury is likely to result

   4.____

5. Steel helmets give workers the MOST protection from

   A. falling objects
   B. eye injuries
   C. fire
   D. electric shock

   5.____

6. It is POOR practice to wear goggles

   A. when chipping stone
   B. when using a grinder
   C. while climbing or descending ladders
   D. when handling molten metal

   6.____

7. When using a brace and bit to bore a hole completely through a partition, it is MOST important to

   7.____

A. lean heavily on the brace and bit
B. maintain a steady turning speed all through the job
C. have the body in a position that will not be easily thrown off balance
D. reverse the direction of the bit at frequent intervals

8. Gloves should be used when handling   8._____

   A. lanterns
   B. wooden rules
   C. heavy ropes
   D. all small tools

Questions 9-16.

DIRECTIONS: Questions 9 through 16, inclusive, are based on the ladder safety rules given below. Read these rules fully before answering these items.

LADDER SAFETY RULES

When a ladder is placed on a slightly uneven supporting surface, use a flat piece of board or small wedge to even up the ladder feet. To secure the proper angle for resting a ladder, it should be placed so that the distance from the base of the ladder to the supporting wall is 1/4 the length of the ladder. To avoid overloading a ladder, only one person should work on a ladder at a time. Do not place a ladder in front of a door. When the top rung of a ladder rests against a pole, the ladder should be lashed securely. Clear loose stones or debris from the ground around the base of a ladder before climbing. While on a ladder, do not attempt to lean so that any part of the body, except arms or hands, extends more than 12 inches beyond the side rail. Always face the ladder when ascending or descending. When carrying ladders through buildings, watch for ceiling globes and lighting fixtures. Avoid the use of rolling ladders as scaffold supports.

9. A small wedge is used to   9._____

   A. even up the feet of a ladder resting on an uneven surface
   B. lock the wheels of a roller ladder
   C. secure the proper resting angle for a ladder
   D. secure a ladder against a pole

10. An 8 foot ladder resting against a wall should be so inclined that the distance between the base of the ladder and the wall is _____ feet.   10._____

    A. 2   B. 5   C. 7   D. 9

11. A ladder should be lashed securely when   11._____

    A. it is placed in front of a door
    B. loose stones are on the ground near the base of the ladder
    C. the top rung rests against a pole
    D. two people are working from the same ladder

12. Rolling ladders   12._____

    A. should be used for scaffold supports
    B. should not be used for scaffold supports
    C. are useful on uneven ground
    D. should be used against a pole

13. When carrying a ladder through a building, it is necessary to

    A. have two men to carry it
    B. carry the ladder vertically
    C. watch for ceiling globes
    D. face the ladder while carrying it

14. It is POOR practice to

    A. lash a ladder securely at any time
    B. clear debris from the base of a ladder before climbing
    C. even up the feet of a ladder resting on slightly uneven ground
    D. place a ladder in front of a door

15. A person on a ladder should NOT extend his head beyond the side rail by more than _____ inches.

    A. 12   B. 9   C. 7   D. 5

16. The MOST important reason for permitting only one person to work on a ladder at a time is that

    A. both could not face the ladder at one time
    B. the ladder will be overloaded
    C. time would be lost going up and down the ladder
    D. they would obstruct each other

17. Many portable electric power tools, such as electric drills, have a third conductor in the power lead which is used to connect the case of the tool to a grounded part of the electric outlet.
    The reason for this extra conductor is to

    A. have a spare wire in case one power wire should break
    B. strengthen the power lead so it cannot easily be damaged
    C. prevent the user of the tool from being shocked
    D. enable the tool to be used for long periods of time without overheating

18. Protective goggles should NOT be worn when

    A. standing on a ladder drilling a steel beam
    B. descending a ladder after completing a job
    C. chipping concrete near a third rail
    D. sharpening a cold chisel on a grinding stone

19. When the foot of an extension ladder, placed against a high wall, rests on a sidewalk or another such similar surface, it is advisable to tie a rope between the bottom rung of the ladder and a point on the wall opposite this rung.
    This is done to prevent

    A. people from walking under the ladder
    B. another worker from removing the ladder
    C. the ladder from vibrating when ascending or descending
    D. the foot of the ladder from slipping

20. In construction work, practically all accidents can be blamed on the

    A. failure of an individual to give close attention to the job assigned to him
    B. use of improper tools
    C. lack of cooperation among the men in a gang
    D. fact that an incompetent man was placed in a key position

21. If it is necessary for you to do some work with your hands under a piece of heavy equipment while a fellow worker lifts up and holds one end of it by means of a pinch bar, one important precaution you should take is to

    A. wear gloves
    B. watch the bar to be ready if it slips
    C. insert a temporary block to support the piece
    D. work as fast as possible

22. Employees of the transit system whose work requires them to enter upon the tracks in the subway are cautioned not to wear loose fitting clothing.
    The MOST important reason for this caution is that loose fitting clothing may

    A. interfere when men are using heavy tools
    B. catch on some projection of a passing train
    C. tear more easily than snug fitting clothing
    D. give insufficient protection against subway dust

23. The MOST important reason for insisting on neatness in maintenance quarters is that it

    A. keeps the men busy in slack periods
    B. prevents tools from becoming rusty
    C. makes a good impression on visitors and officials
    D. decreases the chances of accidents to employees

24. Maintenance workers whose duties require them to do certain types of work generally work in pairs.
    The LEAST likely of the following possible reasons for this practice is that

    A. some of the work requires two men
    B. the men can help each other in case of accident
    C. there is too much equipment for one man to carry
    D. it protects against vandalism

25. A foreman reprimands a helper for actions in violation of the rules and regulations.
    The BEST reaction of the helper in this situation is to

    A. tell the foreman that he was careful and that he did not take any chances
    B. explain that he took this action to save time
    C. keep quiet and accept the criticism
    D. demand that the foreman show him the rule he violated

KEY (CORRECT ANSWERS)

1. A
2. D
3. D
4. D
5. A

6. C
7. C
8. C
9. A
10. A

11. C
12. B
13. C
14. D
15. A

16. B
17. C
18. B
19. D
20. A

21. C
22. B
23. D
24. D
25. C

EXAMINATION SECTION
TEST 1

DIRECTIONS: Each question or incomplete statement is followed by several suggested answers or completions. Select the one that BEST answers the question or completes the statement. *PRINT THE LETTER OF THE CORRECT ANSWER IN THE SPACE AT THE RIGHT.*

1. During an inspection of a plant which manufactures paper products, the officer observes completed work being placed in paper cartons. The cartons are then stacked on wooden skids in a separate storage area awaiting shipment.
The one of the following which is generally the MOST appropriate evaluation of the practice described in this situation is that skids

    A. are highly combustible, adding much fuel to the fire
    B. permit excess air flow to fires
    C. minimize water damage losses by raising stock off the floor
    D. provide space under the stock, thus permitting fire to be more readily extinguished

    1._____

2. Assume that a three-story, Class 3 non-fireproof building has been converted to two-family use. There is one stairway to the street, 2'8" wide. The doors to the apartments all swing in. There are no fire escapes.
The one of the following statements that is MOST accurate is that the situation as described

    A. complies with all applicable laws
    B. is illegal because the stairs are too narrow
    C. is illegal because two means of egress are required
    D. is illegal because the doors do not swing in the direction of egress

    2._____

3. The flammability limits of aviation fuels are of little significance in understanding their fire hazard properties CHIEFLY because the fuels

    A. have practically the same limits
    B. form flammable vapor-air mixtures at all temperatures
    C. ignite readily under tank failure conditions
    D. resist flashing to vapor when in the gelled form

    3._____

4. An inspector enters a luncheonette and discovers that the owner, the only person on duty, apparently does not understand English.
The one of the following which would be the BEST action for the inspector to take in this situation is to attempt to

    A. make the owner understand by speaking English in a loud, clear voice
    B. make the owner understand by using sign language
    C. find a customer or passerby who can act as an interpreter
    D. question the owner closely to determine whether he really does not understand English

    4._____

5. For proper protection of low flash point flammable liquid processes, automatic sprinkler protection with a strong water supply is essential.
The BEST justification of this statement is that

    5._____

11

A. a sprinkler system with a strong water supply will extinguish most fires involving such processes
B. water from sprinklers will reduce the intensity of burning of the liquid and the danger to exposures
C. although the sprinklers are ineffective on flammable liquid fires, they provide protection in the event of other types of fires
D. water from the sprinklers will dilute the flammable liquid and make extinguishment easier

6. According to the regulations, company commanders shall cause a thorough inspection of all schools within their administrative district.
Such inspections shall be made

   A. annually
   B. semi-annually
   C. at the beginning of each school term
   D. within 60 days after school opens for the fall term

6._____

7. While inspecting a garage, a fire inspector notices that a garage license has not been issued for the premises by the Department of Licenses.
The inspector should

   A. discontinue his inspection pending a determination by the Department of Licenses of the allowable motor vehicle occupancy
   B. complete his inspection and forward it (including a statement of the allowable motor vehicle occupancy) with a request that a copy be sent to the Department of Licenses
   C. discontinue his inspection and request that a communication (inquiry form) be sent to the Department of Licenses asking for an explanation
   D. complete his inspection and forward it with a request that the Department of Licenses be asked to determine the allowable motor vehicle occupancy

7._____

Questions 8-11.

DIRECTIONS: Questions 8 through 11 are to be answered on the basis of the information given in the following paragraph.

The principal value of inspection work is in the knowledge obtained relating to the various structural features of the building and the protective features provided. Knowledge of the location of stairways and elevators, the obstruction provided by merchandise, the danger from absorption of water by baled stock, the potential hazard of rupture of containers such as drums or cylinders, and the location of protective equipment, all are essential features to be noted and later discussed in company school and officer's college.

8. According to the above paragraph, the CHIEF value of inspection work is to gather information which will aid in

   A. fixing responsibility for fires
   B. planning firefighting operations
   C. training new firemen
   D. obtaining compliance with the Building Code

8._____

9. The one of the following objects which would be the MOST help in accomplishing the objective of the inspection as stated in the above paragraph is a

   A. copy of the Building Code
   B. chemical analysis kit
   C. plan of the building
   D. list of the building's tenants

10. An example of a *structural feature* contained in the above paragraph is the

    A. location of stairways and elevators
    B. obstruction provided by merchandise
    C. danger of absorption of water by baled stock
    D. hazard of rupture of containers such as drums or cylinders

11. Of the following, the BEST example of what is meant by a *protective feature,* as used in the above paragraph, is

    A. a fire extinguisher
    B. a burglar alarm
    C. fire insurance
    D. a medical first-aid kit

12. When a violation order is to be served and the owner or person in charge of the premises cannot readily be located, every effort shall be made to serve such order. Of the following statements concerning the attempts to serve such an order, the one that is NOT correct is:

    A. Attempt to ascertain from occupants or people in the area the name and address of the owner or management
    B. Send a member to effect service if the owner or management is located in the city but out of the company district
    C. Make an appointment by telephone for service of the order
    D. Post the violation notice prominently in or on the premises and mail a copy to the owner or management

13. Every applicant for a certificate of license to install underground gasoline storage tanks is required to

    A. be a resident of the city and maintain a place of business in the city
    B. file a bond and evidence of liability insurance
    C. be a resident of the city or maintain a place of business in the city
    D. pass a written examination given by the fire department

14. The Fire Prevention Code specifies that a special permit is required for each of the following EXCEPT

    A. refining petroleum collected from oil separators or manufacturing plants
    B. loading of small arms ammunition by hand in a retail store selling ammunition
    C. operating a wholesale drug or chemical house
    D. generating acetylene gas

15. The one of the following that is the MOST acceptable statement concerning the fire protection for the truck loading rack in a bulk oil terminal is that the rack must be equipped with a

A. water spray system, automatically controlled
B. foam system, remote manually controlled
C. water spray system, remote manually controlled
D. foam system, automatically controlled

16. The one of the following which is NOT in accord with the regulations for the use of Halon 1301, extinguishing agent, is that

    A. maximum concentration shall not exceed 10 percent where human habitation is present in the volume to be flooded
    B. minimum concentration of FE 1301 used shall not be less than 10 percent
    C. a discharge rate which results in attaining the design concentration in 8 seconds is acceptable
    D. a central office connection must be provided for fire detection or systems operating where human habitation is present in the volume to be flooded

17. Members of the uniformed force are authorized to issue summonses where fire perils exist, although it is generally preferable to first issue a violation order to correct the illegal condition.
    However, members must issue a summons immediately in a licensed place of public assembly upon noting

    A. an obstructed revolving exit door in a crowded cabaret
    B. the absence of a certified standpipe system operator in a theatre
    C. an inoperative fire extinguishing system in a restaurant cooking duct
    D. standees in a motion picture theatre

18. During the course of an inspection at a blasting site, an officer notes that the magazine has been provided with electrical security devices, and that it contains eight 10-pound cartons of explosives which are to be stored overnight, overhead wires run from the magazine to the watchman's shanty, and the driller, without a C. of F., loads holes under the direct supervision of the blaster. The condition as described is generally ILLEGAL because

    A. explosives must be in original and unbroken packages of 50 or 25 pound capacity only
    B. storage of explosives between the hours of 10 P.M. and 6 A.M. is prohibited
    C. all electrical wiring must be protected by heavy wall conduit and be buried at least 12 inches deep
    D. no person may load holes in blasting operations unless they hold a certificate of fitness

19. The one of the following that is LEAST in accord with the regulations for the use of Halon 1301 extinguishing agent systems is that

    A. these systems are limited to applications as automatic total flooding systems for interior Class B and C fires and Class A fires that are not deep-seated
    B. abort systems are permitted for smoke detector activated systems which provide the manual capacity to *dump* the Halon 1301 immediately
    C. actuation of only one products-of-combustion device will fail to initiate the *dump* of Halon 1301 but will actuate the local and central office company alarms
    D. concentrations used shall not exceed 10 percent in areas where human habitation is present in the volume to be flooded

5 (#1)

20. Interstate transportation of petroleum products into and through the city in tank trucks which do NOT conform to fire department requirements is GENERALLY

    A. *not permitted* even when the pickups are all made outside the city and no pickups are made in the city
    B. *permitted* without restriction if the vehicles comply with United States Department of Transportation regulations governing interstate commerce
    C. *not permitted* where deliveries are to be made in the city
    D. *permitted* during non-business hours, along regularly established commercial routes

20.____

21. Of the following occupancies constructed and occupied in 1962, each of which accommodates less than 300 persons, the one that CANNOT be described as a *place of assembly,* according to the applicable building code, is a

    A. college assembly hall
    B. motion picture theatre
    C. courtroom
    D. legitimate theatre

21.____

22. According to the labor law, the one of the following conditions that is generally considered to be LEGAL in a 5-story building constructed and occupied as a factory since 1911 is that

    A. a single means of egress is provided from a floor of 2500 sq.ft. or less where no person is regularly employed
    B. no point on the upper floor which is equipped with an approved sprinkler system is more than 200 feet distant from an exit
    C. one of the two required stairways extends to the roof from which there is egress to an adjacent building
    D. there are double swinging doors leading to an exit on an upper floor where more than 5 persons are employed

22.____

23. Certain old factory buildings may be found to have some fire escapes which are not in accordance with the requirements of the labor law.
It is generally CORRECT to state of these substandard factory exits that they

    A. may be used in computing occupancy exit requirements if maintained in good repair and the building is equipped with an automatic sprinkler
    B. must be provided with a counterbalanced stairway in lieu of the former drop ladder in guides
    C. shall be kept clear of all obstructions and periodically used during required fire drills
    D. may not be equipped with any exit or directional sign at the openings leading thereto

23.____

24. According to the labor law, the use of plate glass in fire windows in fireproof buildings is

    A. *prohibited,* except in buildings less than 75 feet in height
    B. *permitted,* if the fire windows are located more than 30 feet horizontally from the nearest opening in the wall of another building
    C. *prohibited* for use in all fire windows in fireproof buildings
    D. *permitted* if the fire windows are more than 30 feet above the roof of a building within a horizontal distance of 25 feet

24.____

25. Under certain conditions, a newsstand may be located in a street floor lobby which serves as an exit passageway for a building constructed after 1976.
The one of the following which is NOT one of these conditions is that the newsstand must

    A. occupy no more than 100 square feet or 5 percent of the net floor area of the lobby, whichever is greater
    B. not reduce the clear width of the lobby at any point
    C. be located at least 30 feet from an exit door
    D. be protected by at least 2 automatic sprinkler heads if constructed of combustible material

---

KEY (CORRECT ANSWERS)

1.	C	11.	A
2.	A	12.	D
3.	C	13.	C
4.	C	14.	D
5.	B	15.	C
6.	A	16.	B
7.	D	17.	C
8.	B	18.	D
9.	C	19.	D
10.	A	20.	D

21. C
22. B
23. A
24. B
25. B

TEST 2

DIRECTIONS: Each question or incomplete statement is followed by several suggested answers or completions. Select the one that BEST answers the question or completes the statement. *PRINT THE LETTER OF THE CORRECT ANSWER IN THE SPACE AT THE RIGHT.*

1. Suppose that a factory has stored within it a number of substances. 1.____
   If the owner asked you which of the following is MOST likely to constitute a fire hazard, you would reply

   A. sodium chloride
   B. calcium chloride
   C. chromium
   D. silicon dioxide

2. Vertical openings, such as dumbwaiters, elevators, and chutes, are the bane of a fire- 2.____
   fighting force.
   This condition arises MAINLY because the existence of such openings in a burning building facilitates

   A. accidental falls
   B. generation of gases
   C. spread of the fire
   D. the perpetration of arson

3. Suppose that a neighbor were to ask you whether there is more hazard in the use of ker- 3.____
   osene than gasoline at ordinary room temperature.
   You should reply that there is MORE hazard in the use of

   A. *kerosene*, because it gives off dangerous quantities of explosive vapors which are lighter than air
   B. *gasoline*, because gasoline vapor may flow along the floor and be ignited at a long distance from its point of origin
   C. *kerosene*, because its flash point is very low
   D. *gasoline*, particularly because when ignited it burns

4. Steel supporting beams in buildings often are surrounded by a thin layer of concrete to 4.____
   keep the beams from becoming hot and collapsing during a fire.
   The one of the following statements which BEST explains how collapse is prevented by this arrangement is that concrete

   A. becomes stronger as its temperature is increased
   B. acts as an insulating material
   C. protects the beam from rust and corrosion
   D. reacts chemically with steel at high temperatures

5. It has been suggested that property owners should be charged a fee each time the Fire 5.____
   Department is called to extinguish a fire on their property.
   Of the following, the BEST reason for *rejecting* this proposal is that

   A. delay in calling the Fire Department may result
   B. many property owners don't occupy the property they own
   C. property owners may resent such a charge as they pay real estate taxes
   D. it may be difficult to determine on whose property a fire started

6. An officer inspecting buildings in a commercial area came to one whose outside surface appeared to be of natural stone. The owner told the officer that it was not necessary to inspect his building as it was *fireproof.* The officer, however, completed his inspection of the building.
   Of the following, the BEST reason for continuing the inspection is that

   A. stone buildings catch fire as readily as wooden buildings
   B. the Fire Department cannot make exceptions in its inspection procedures
   C. the building may have been built of imitation stone
   D. interiors and contents of stone buildings can catch fire

7. From the viewpoint of fire safety, the CHIEF advantage of a foam rubber mattress compared to a cotton mattress is that the foam rubber mattress

   A. is slower burning
   B. generates less heat when burning
   C. does not smolder
   D. is less subject to water damage

8. At a social gathering, a fire chief hears a man who describes himself as the owner of the XYZ factory state that he *pays off* fire department inspectors who visit his establishment. When the chief asks the man whether he will repeat his statement under oath, the man refuses with the remark, *I am not looking for trouble.*
   In this situation, the chief should

   A. forget the incident since the factory owner is not willing to give evidence
   B. investigate the background and reputation of the man to determine whether he really owns the factory and has any reason for making false statements about the fire department
   C. report the incident to police authorities
   D. report the incident to higher authorities in the fire department

9. The one of the following methods of storing large piles of coal which is undesirable because it increases the danger of spontaneous heating is

   A. making the pile compact by use of a roller
   B. storing the coal on smooth, solid ground
   C. covering the sides and top of the pile with road tar
   D. mixing coal of various sizes in one pile

10. The one of the following materials which has the LEAST tendency to spontaneous heating is

    A. baled hides
    B. bagged charcoal
    C. bulk fish scrap
    D. boxed mineral wool

11. In most buildings in which lighting is provided by artificial means and an auxiliary system for emergency exit lighting is not provided, phosphorescent exit and directional signs are required.
    Of the following occupancies, the one which is generally EXCLUDED from this requirement is a

    A. warehouse
    B. school dormitory
    C. hospital
    D. library

12. In determining overcrowding or adequacy of means of egress, a fire officer must be aware that the minimum number of persons to be provided for in any floor area shall be the number which can be accommodated within the net floor area at a given occupancy and area per person.
Accordingly, the GREATEST concentration of persons to be provided for will be generally found in a

    A. basement sales area
    B. high school classroom
    C. dance hall
    D. work room

13. Of the following statements, the one that is generally ACCURATE concerning the installation of combustible luminous suspended ceilings is that they may

    A. not be installed below an existing suspended ceiling
    B. be installed below existing sprinkler heads
    C. not be used in any room in occupancy group F (assembly)
    D. be installed in corridors not exceeding 100 sq.ft.

14. The building code exempts from the sprinkler requirements those floors which are generally unventilated but are equipped with a given openable area.
A fixed window will be considered openable if it is

    A. equipped with an interior heat sensitive device to actuate the automatic fire shutters
    B. of frangible glass panels and located 15 feet below grade
    C. within 8 feet of an openable window of at least 3 feet x 3 feet dimension
    D. readily broken and not more than 110 feet above grade

15. Of the following, the MOST complete and accurate statement about exit requirements is that there shall be at least two door openings, remote from each other and leading to exits from every room or enclosed space, in a business occupancy (E) in which the total occupant load *exceeds*

    A. 25   B. 50   C. 75   D. 100

16. On October 23, 1976, 25 persons died and many were injured as a result of an arson fire in an illegal social club in the Bronx.
Of the following, the MOST probable contributory cause of this multiple loss of life was the

    A. door to the club was not self-closing and was opened in the direction of egress when the fire occurred
    B. front windows had been bricked-up and prevented access by department ladders
    C. confusing layout caused many patrons to bypass the secondary means of egress and become trapped in the toilet rooms
    D. original lath and plaster had been replaced by combustible wood paneling and there had been an extensive use of highly flammable decorations

17. It is INCORRECT for a fire officer giving training on the protection of electronic data processing (EDP) units and ancillary equipment against fire damage to state that

A. the design features of EDP units make them relatively resistant to damage by temperatures under 600° F
B. smoke and acids produced by fire can adversely affect the operation of computer equipment and magnetic components
C. the heat and steam produced by a fire and its extinguishment that would not normally damage ordinary paper records may easily damage magnetic tapes
D. in cases where fire can spread throughout or beyond the computer's housing, a fixed CO_2 system may be required

18. Of the following exit and access requirements relating to dead-end corridors in various occupancy group buildings, it is generally MOST accurate to state that

    A. no more than one classroom shall be permitted on a dead-end corridor in an educational occupancy
    B. storage of combustible materials in non-combustible lockers is permitted in dead-end corridors in an institutional occupancy
    C. dead-end corridors are not permitted in an assembly occupancy
    D. no more than one patient bedroom is permitted in a dead-end corridor in an institutional occupancy

19. In the past, building marquee collapses have resulted in the injury or death of firefighters. According to the new building code, marquees are generally

    A. not permitted
    B. permitted if supported by incombustible piers at the curb line
    C. not permitted to project beyond the street line
    D. permitted on buildings of a public nature but may have to be removed if the building occupancy is changed

20. When a standpipe system is altered, extended, or extensively repaired, it must undergo certain inspections and tests.
    Of the following, it is generally MOST accurate to state that the

    A. entire system shall be subjected to the hydrostatic test pressure
    B. altered, new or repaired section shall be subjected to the pressure test and the entire system subjected to the flow test
    C. flow test shall be confined to a determination that water is available at the top outlet of each riser
    D. pressure test in buildings not exceeding 3 stories or 40 feet in height need only sustain 150 percent of the normal hydrostatic pressure at the topmost hose outlet

21. A substance which is subject to *spontaneous combustion* is one that

    A. is explosive when heated
    B. is capable of catching fire without an external source of heat
    C. acts to speed up the burning of material
    D. liberates oxygen when heated

Questions 22-25.

DIRECTIONS: Questions 22 through 25 are to be answered on the basis of the following paragraph.

For the five-year period 2006-2010, inclusive, the average annual fire loss in the United States amounted to approximately $1,354,830,000. Included in this estimate is $1,072,666,000 damage to buildings and contents, and $282,164,000 average annual loss in aircraft, motor vehicles, forest and other miscellaneous fires not involving buildings. Preliminary estimates indicate that the total United States fire loss in 2011 was $1,615,000,000. These are property damage fire losses only and do not include indirect losses resulting from fires which are just as real and sometimes far more serious than property damage losses. But because evaluation of indirect monetary losses is usually very difficult, their importance in the national fire waste picture is often overlooked.

22. According to the data in the above paragraph, the BEST of the following estimates of the total direct fire loss in the United States for the six-year period 2006-2011, inclusive, is

   A. $1,400,000,000
   B. $2,700,000,000
   C. $7,000,000,000
   D. $8,400,000,000

23. The BEST example of an indirect fire loss, as that term is used in the above paragraph, is monetary loss due to

   A. smoke or water damage to exposures
   B. condemnation of foodstuffs following a fire
   C. interruption of business following a fire
   D. forcible entry by firemen operating at a fire

24. Suppose that during the period 2011-2015 the average annual fire loss to buildings and contents increases 10 percent, and the average annual loss due to fires not involving buildings decreases 10 percent. The MOST valid of the following conclusions is that the average annual fire loss for the 2011-2015 period, compared to the losses for the 2006-2011 period,

   A. will increase
   B. will decrease
   C. will be unchanged
   D. cannot be calculated from the information given

25. If a comparison is made between total annual direct and indirect fire losses on the basis of the information given in the above paragraph, the MOST valid of the following conclusions is that

   A. generally, direct losses are higher
   B. generally, indirect losses are higher
   C. generally, direct and indirect losses are approximately equal
   D. there is not sufficient information to determine which is higher or if they are approximately equal

KEY (CORRECT ANSWERS)

1. D
2. C
3. B
4. B
5. A

6. D
7. C
8. D
9. D
10. D

11. D
12. A
13. C
14. A
15. D

16. A
17. C
18. A
19. D
20. C

21. B
22. D
23. C
24. A
25. D

TEST 3

DIRECTIONS: Each question or incomplete statement is followed by several suggested answers or completions. Select the one that BEST answers the question or completes the statement. *PRINT THE LETTER OF THE CORRECT ANSWER IN THE SPACE AT THE RIGHT.*

1. It has been suggested that companies be given additional Apparatus Field Inspection Duty and other inspectional duties as punishment for poor performance of evolutions, poor condition of equipment or quarters, etc.
Of the following, the MOST valid objection to this proposal is that

    A. the punishment does not directly improve the skills or functions which are found to be deficient
    B. inspectional activities would be degraded by making such assignments a form of punishment
    C. the punishment is imposed on a group rather than on an individual basis
    D. scheduling of regular inspectional activities would be disrupted

2. The Administrative Code authorizes members to issue summonses in cases arising under laws relating to fires and to fire peril.
Departmental regulations require that such summonses be returnable in the appropriate court _____ than 14 calendar days, _____ Sundays and holidays.

    A. not less; including
    B. not less; excluding
    C. not more; including
    D. not more; excluding

3. When conducting an Apparatus Field Inspection of an occupancy with a required and approved sprinkler system, it is MOST important, of the following, for firemen to make certain that

    A. feeder lines are adequate to supply the number of sprinkler heads
    B. sprinkler heads are sufficient and properly spaced
    C. stock does not interfere with the proper distribution of water from sprinkler heads
    D. records of monthly hydrostatic pressure tests are properly kept and are up to date

4. While inspecting an above-ground storage tank installation, an inspector notices leakage of the contents through *weep* holes in a tank.
This is a sign that the

    A. tank contents are under excessive pressure
    B. strength of the entire tank may be endangered by corrosion
    C. volumetric capacity of the tank has been exceeded
    D. tank is *breathing* as intended

5. A member on inspectional duty came across, in a building under construction, a propane gas heater with its safety valve negated by means of wire and tape across the buttons at the top of the safety assembly.
Of the following actions taken by the member in this situation, the one that is NOT in accord with departmental orders is the

A. serving of a violation order to discontinue use of devices to negate safety features on propane gas heaters on premises
B. picking up of the permits for storage and use of propane
C. notification of the Battalion Chief of the administrative district concerned
D. impounding of the propane heater

6. Of the following, the PRIMARY purpose of holding fire tests at a high-rise office building is to

    A. determine the hazard of polyurethane insulation
    B. evaluate the effectiveness of sprinklers with a limited water supply
    C. test the effectiveness of stair pressurization
    D. develop procedures for venting the fire floor by window vents

7. At the first sign of a fire, the manager of a motion picture theatre had the lights turned on and made the following announcement: *Ladies and gentlemen, the management has found it necessary to dismiss the audience. Please remain seated until it is time for your aisle to file out. In leaving the theatre, follow the directions of the ushers. There is no danger involved.*
The manager's action in this situation was

    A. *proper*
    B. *improper,* chiefly because he did not tell the audience the reason for the dismissal
    C. *improper,* chiefly because he did not permit all members of the audience to leave at once
    D. *improper,* chiefly because he misled the audience by saying that there was no danger

8. Generally, sprinkler heads must be replaced each time they are used.
The BEST explanation of why this is necessary is that the sprinkler heads

    A. are subject to rusting after discharging water
    B. may become clogged after discharging water
    C. have a distorted pattern of discharge of water after use
    D. are set off by the effect of heat on metal and cannot be reset

9. A fire insurance inspector suggested to the manager of a fireproof warehouse that bags of flour be stacked on skids (wooden platforms 6" high, 6x6 feet in area). Of the following, the BEST justification for this suggestion is that in the event of a fire, the bags on skids are less likely to

    A. topple
    B. be damaged by water used in extinguishment
    C. catch fire
    D. be ripped by fire equipment

10. Permitting piles of scrap paper cuttings to accumulate in a factory building is a bad practice CHIEFLY because they may

    A. ignite spontaneously
    B. interfere with fire extinguishment operations
    C. catch fire from a spark or smoldering match
    D. interfere with escape of occupants if a fire occurs

11. High grass and weeds should not be permitted to grow near a building CHIEFLY because, in the event of a grass fire, the weeds and grass may

    A. give off toxic fumes
    B. limit maneuverability of firemen
    C. interfere with the escape of occupants from the building
    D. bring the fire to the building and set it on fire

12. Visitors near patients in *oxygen tents* are not permitted to smoke.
    The BEST of the following reasons for this prohibition is that

    A. the flame of the cigarette or cigar may flare dangerously
    B. smoking tobacco is irritating to persons with respiratory disease
    C. smoking in bed is one of the major causes of fires
    D. diseases may be transmitted by means of tobacco smoke

13. A MAJOR difference between the building code currently in effect and the one in effect prior to it is that in the current code

    A. doors to the outside grade must be the same size as corridor doors
    B. sprinklering of a building will permit a reduction in total door width
    C. the width of an exit door is based on the width of the corridor leading to it
    D. the width of exit doors is based on both the number of persons and the type of occupancy

14. While inspecting a one-story factory building erected in 1962, you notice that an exit door has been relocated. The size, location, and lighting of all exits in the building comply with the old building code in effect before.
    To determine whether the relocated exit is a legal one, it is necessary to check the provisions of

    A. the State Labor Law and the new building code for the relocated exit *only*
    B. the State Labor Law *only*
    C. the new building code for the relocated exit *only*
    D. none of the foregoing since checking the old building code is sufficient

15. The new building code divides the construction clauses into two major construction groups.
    These two groups are called

    A. fireproof and non-fireproof
    B. rigid frame and flexible frame
    C. commercial and residential
    D. combustible and noncombustible

16. The State Labor Law requires that the balconies and stairways of outside fire escapes be able to safely sustain a live load, in pounds per square foot, of _____ with a safety factor of _____.

    A. 75; two   B. 90; four   C. 105; two   D. 120; four

17. A plant manufacturing nitro-cellulose products has 100 employees. The Fire Prevention Code requires that these premises be equipped with fire pails filled with water. The required MINIMUM number of such pails must be

    A. 25 B. 50 C. 75 D. 100

18. The MAIN purpose of an oil separator is to

    A. separate volatile inflammable oils from other oils
    B. provide a fireproof block between a spark or flame device and an oil storage tank
    C. prevent volatile inflammable oils from flowing into a sewer
    D. make it impossible for the wrong kind of oil to be delivered from a bulk storage plant

19. The MAXIMUM quantity of fuel oil permitted to be stored in an exposed tank in the cellar of a two-family dwelling is _____ gallons.

    A. 225 B. 550 C. 750 D. 875

20. According to the Fire Prevention Code, the MAXIMUM quantity of paint (other than water base) that may be stored without a permit is _____ gallons.

    A. 10 B. 15 C. 20 D. 25

21. Of the following licenses, certificates of qualification, or certificates of fitness, the Fire Department does NOT issue the one authorizing the holder to

    A. operate refrigerating machines (unlimited capacity)
    B. install underground storage tanks for gasoline
    C. operate low pressure boilers using #6 oil
    D. install oil burning equipment

22. In the course of your work in a residential area, you see a wood frame, brick veneer dwelling, two-stories and attic in height, erected in 1965. The building is occupied by two families, with a living room in the attic.
    Without special approval by the Board of Standards and Appeals, this condition could

    A. not be legal
    B. be legal provided that there is a fire escape from the attic
    C. be legal provided the stair enclosure is properly fire retarded
    D. be legal provided that the attic living room is not used as a bedroom

23. A typical occupancy falling into the Assembly occupancy group as used in the building code would be a

    A. radio station   B. library
    C. nursing home   D. tavern

24. Of the following situations, the one in which a fire escape may NOT be considered a legal means of egress is in a three-story

    A. factory building erected in 1912
    B. mixed occupancy building with a store on the first floor and one family on each of the floors above, erected in 1965
    C. multiple dwelling erected in 1971
    D. office building erected in 1950 and altered in 1972

25. A storage garage is one that has
    A. a stock room for repair parts for vehicles
    B. an area for vehicles that are not used on a daily basis
    C. a gasoline tank to supply gasoline to the vehicles
    D. room only for vehicles that are to be sold

25.____

KEY (CORRECT ANSWERS)

1. B
2. A
3. C
4. B
5. A

6. C
7. A
8. D
9. B
10. C

11. D
12. A
13. D
14. B
15. D

16. B
17. B
18. C
19. B
20. C

21. D
22. A
23. D
24. C
25. C

TEST 4

DIRECTIONS: Each question or incomplete statement is followed by several suggested answers or completions. Select the one that BEST answers the question or completes the statement. *PRINT THE LETTER OF THE CORRECT ANSWER IN THE SPACE AT THE RIGHT.*

1. A violation order is to be served requiring the immediate removal of liquefied petroleum gas cylinders when such cylinders are found on construction sites without a permit issued by the Fire Department.
Pending removal of such cylinders,

    A. vacate procedures are to be instituted
    B. a fireman is to be detailed to the site to safeguard the illegally stored gas cylinders
    C. the contractor is to be ordered to provide a watchman to safeguard the illegally stored gas cylinders
    D. the Police Department is to be notified so that a patrolman can be assigned to the site to safeguard the illegally stored gas cylinders

2. A four-story loft building is now occupied as follows: Street level - furniture repair and refinishing shop; 2nd story - one apartment occupied by an artist-in-residence, wife, and 5 young children; 3rd story - two apartments each occupied by an artist-in-residence and his wife; 4th story - one apartment occupied by an artist-in-residence, his wife, and his mother-in-law. The building is non-fireproof construction, 40' x 70', is 50' in height, and has an automatic wet sprinkler system protecting the furniture shop. The occupancy as described is

    A. *legal*
    B. *illegal,* because the sprinkler system does not extend throughout the building
    C. *illegal,* because the number of occupants exceeds the permissible limits
    D. *illegal,* because of the presence of the furniture repair and refinishing shop

3. Some organizations have adopted the National Fire Protection Association diamond-shaped coding system for identifying characteristics of hazardous materials. The diamond shown in the diagram at the right has its boxes labeled W, X, Y, and Z.
Under the National Fire Protection Association coding system, the lettered boxes represent, respectively,

    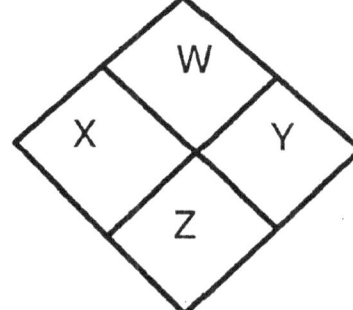

    A. X - Health, Y - Reactive, W - Flammable
    B. X - Reactive, Y - Flammable, W - Health
    C. X - Health, Y - Reactive, Z - Flammable
    D. X - Flammable, Y - Health, Z - Reactive

4. The shut sprinkler control valve is one of industry's greatest fire hazards. When it is necessary to shut down a system for repairs or other reasons, certain precautions should be taken.
Of the following statements regarding such precautions, the LEAST acceptable is to

   A. have the system shut down during non-working hours
   B. have the system shut down during working hours while normal operations are going on
   C. notify the Fire Department of the intended shutdown
   D. prepare to supply the system through the two-inch drain in the event of an emergency or fire

Questions 5-8.

DIRECTIONS: Questions 5 through 8 are to be answered on the basis of the information given in the following paragraph.

A mixture of a combustible vapor and air will burn only when the proportion of fuel to air lies within a certain range, i.e., between the upper and lower limits of flammability. If a third, non-combustible gas is now added to the mixture, the limits will be narrowed. As increasing amounts of diluent are added, the limits come closer until, at a certain critical concentration, they will converge. This is the peak concentration. It is the minimum amount of diluent that will inhibit the combustion of any fuel-air mixture.

5. If additional diluent is added beyond the peak concentration, the flammable limits of the mixture will

   A. converge rapidly
   B. diverge slowly
   C. diverge rapidly
   D. not be affected

6. If the four numbers listed below were peak concentration values obtained in a test of four diluents, then the MOST efficient diluent would have the value of

   A. 7.5   B. 10   C. 12.5   D. 15

7. The word *inhibit,* as used in the last sentence of the above paragraph, means MOST NEARLY

   A. slow the rate of
   B. prevent entirely the occurrence of
   C. reduce the intensity of
   D. retard to an appreciable extent the manifestation of

8. The one of the graphs shown below which BEST represents the process described in the paragraph is

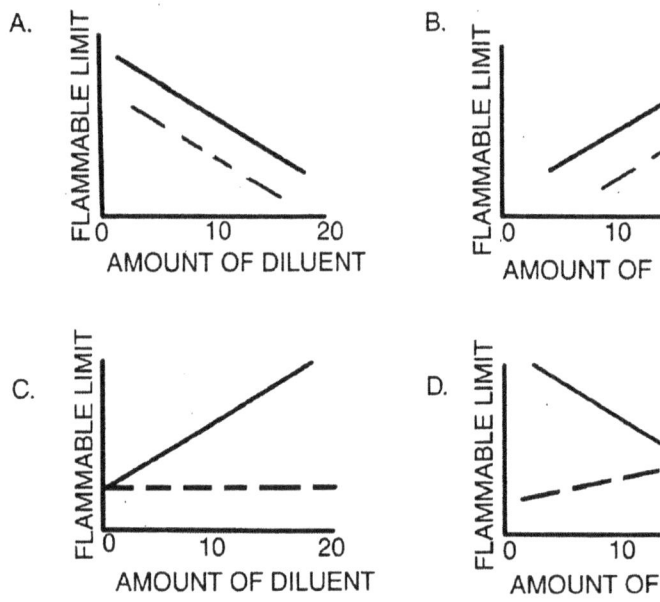

———————— UPPER FLAMMABLE LIMITS

— — — — — — LOWER FLAMMABLE LIMITS

9. Of the following metals, the one which is LEAST acceptable as a non-sparking metal for tools is

   A. hardened copper
   B. bronze
   C. brass
   D. copper alloys

10. Of the heating defects responsible for hotel fires, the MAJOR defect is

    A. defective flues
    B. overheated appliances
    C. defective appliances
    D. inadequate clearance

11. Community relations and fire prevention education efforts must be concentrated in residential neighborhoods, particularly in the depressed areas of the city.
    The one of the following which does NOT provide support for this point of view is that

    A. residential occupants are exposed to more serious occupancy hazards than industrial workers
    B. open hydrants, excessive false alarms, and hostile acts are concentrated in depressed areas
    C. rubbish fires and vacant building fires are most frequent in these areas
    D. the primary incidence of fire takes place in residential areas

12. The State Multiple Dwelling Law allows a *family* to have four boarders, and the City Multiple Dwelling Law allows a *family* to have only two boarders.
    In the city, a *family* is allowed

A. two boarders because the Multiple Dwelling Code is the more restrictive requirement
B. four boarders because the State law takes precedence over the city code
C. two or four boarders, depending upon whether the Law or Code applies to a given situation
D. two or four boarders, at the discretion of the Fire Commissioner

13. Fire Department regulations governing the issuance of city-wide permits for the use of combustible gases during temporary torch operations require fire guards to make inspections after completion of torch operations for the purpose of detecting fire. Signed inspection reports are to be filed and available for examination by the Fire Department.
The one of the following which is MOST accurate and complete is that such inspections are to be made _____ after completion of operations.

A. every 15 minutes, for a period of one hour,
B. one-half hour and one hour
C. every half hour, for a period of two hours,
D. one half hour, one hour, and two hours,

14. On an A.F.I.D., a company comes upon the following garages:
   I. Adjacent to a dwelling occupied by one family, storing two cars, one owned by the family and the other by the next door neighbor who pays a monthly rental
   II. In a dwelling outside the fire limits, occupied by one family storing three cars owned by the family
   III. In a fireproof dwelling occupied by three families in two stories above the garage, with two means of egress and no entrances to any apartment through the garage, storing two cars owned by tenants
A Fire Department permit is required for

A. none of these garages
B. garages I and III
C. garages II and III
D. all three garages

15. If a building is altered under the provisions of the building code, and the building is not provided with sprinkler protection, the one of the following actions that the company officer should take is to

A. transmit an A-8 report for referral to the Department of Buildings
B. issue a summons to the owner of the building
C. prepare a report on Department letterhead and send it to the Division of Fire Prevention
D. call the Department of Buildings and notify them about the violation

16. The one of the following fibers that can be made into fabric which can be effectively treated with common water-soluble-salt flame-retardant solutions is

A. dacron
B. nylon
C. rayon
D. nomex

17. The inspection of public assembly occupancies classified as theatres in company administrative districts should be scheduled so that each such premises is inspected AT LEAST once every

A. 30 days, approximately one half hour before scheduled performances
B. 30 days, at irregular time periods when premises are open to the public

C. three months, approximately one half hour before scheduled performances
D. three months, at irregular time periods when premises are open to the public

18. The one of the following automatic fire alarm detectors that works on the principle of uneven expansion of bi-metallic strips is the _____ device.

    A. rate compensation
    B. ionization type
    C. rate of rise type
    D. fixed temperature

18._____

19. The one of the following which is probably the MOST frequent source of ignition of flammable vapors in hospital operating rooms is

    A. static electricity
    B. x-ray equipment
    C. sterilizing machinery
    D. electric cauterizing devices

19._____

20. At an open demonstration, polyurethane foam, widely used in furniture, was exposed to fire.
    In this demonstration, it was shown that the foam

    A. was self-extinguishing
    B. flamed and gave off acrid smoke
    C. could not be ignited
    D. melted but would not flame

20._____

Questions 21-23.

DIRECTIONS: Questions 21 through 23 are to be answered on the basis of the following paragraph.

Shafts extending into the top story, except those stair shafts where the stairs do not continue to the roof, shall be carried through and at least two feet above the roof. Every shaft extending above the roof, except open shafts and elevator shafts, shall be enclosed at the top with a roof of materials having a fire resistive rating of one hour and a metal skylight covering at least three-quarters of the area of the shaft in the top story, except that skylights over stair shafts shall have an area not less than one-tenth the area of the shaft in the top story, but shall be not less than fifteen square feet in area. Any shaft terminating below the top story of a structure and those stair shafts not required to extend through the roof shall have the top enclosed with materials having the same fire resistive rating as required for the shaft enclosure.

21. The above paragraph states that the elevator shafts which extend into the top story are

    A. not required to have a skylight but are required to extend at least two feet above the roof
    B. neither required to have a skylight nor to extend above the roof
    C. required to have a skylight covering at least three-quarters of the area of the shaft in the top story and to extend at least two feet above the roof
    D. required to have a skylight covering at least three-quarters of the area of the shaft in the top story but are not required to extend above the roof

21._____

22. The one of the following skylights which meets the requirements of the above paragraph is a skylight measuring

    A. 4' x 4' over a stair shaft which, on the top story, measures 20' x 9'
    B. 4 1/2' x 3 1/2' over a pipe shaft which, on the top story, measures 5' x 4'
    C. 2 1/2' x 1 1/2' over a dumbwaiter shaft which, on the top story, measures 2 1/2' x 2 1/2'
    D. 4' x 3' over a stair shaft which, on the top story, measures 15' x 6'

23. Suppose that in a Class I building, a shaft which does not go to the roof is required to have a three-hour fire resistive rating.
    In regard to the material enclosing the top of this shaft, the above paragraph

    A. states that a one-hour fire resistive rating is required
    B. states that a three-hour fire resistive rating is required
    C. implies that no fire resistive rating is required
    D. neither states nor implies anything about the fire resistive rating

Questions 24-25.

DIRECTIONS: Questions 24 and 25 are to be answered SOLELY on the basis of the following passage.

The four different types of building collapses are as follows:

1. <u>Building Wall Collapse</u> - An outside wall of the building collapses but the floors maintain their positions.

2. <u>Lean-to Collapse</u> - One end of a floor collapses onto the floor below it. This leaves a sheltered area on the floor below.

3. <u>Floor Collapse</u> - An entire floor falls to the floor below it but large pieces of machinery in the floor below provide spaces which can provide shelter.

4. <u>Pancake Collapse</u> - A floor collapses completely onto the floor below it, leaving no spaces. In some cases, the force of this collapse causes successive lower floors to collapse.

24. The MOST serious injuries are likely to occur at _____ collapses.

    A. pancake   B. lean-to
    C. floor   D. building wall

25. Of the following, a floor collapse is MOST likely to occur in a(n)

    A. apartment building   B. private home
    C. factory building   D. hotel

26. When using a standardized survey report during AFID, it generally is NOT advisable to make an inspection of the facilities in the strict sequence of the items on the form PRIMARILY because the

    A. sequence of the items in the form may not correspond to the physical arrangement of the occupancy or structure
    B. members performing inspection duty will be more likely to make errors of omission rather than commission on the forms

C. occupancy or structure may require a multi-inspector, multi-page form inspectional approach
D. procedure does not permit distribution of tasks among all the members participating in the inspection

27. Sparks given off by welding torches are a serious fire hazard.
The BEST of the following methods of dealing with this hazard is to conduct welding operations only

   A. in fireproof buildings protected by sprinkler systems
   B. out-of-doors on a day with little wind blowing
   C. on materials certified to be non-combustible by recognized testing laboratories
   D. after loose combustible materials have been cleared from the area and with a man standing by with a hose line

28. Two types of steel hoops are commonly found on older wooden gravity tanks - round hoops and flat ones.
The one of the following statements concerning such hoops that is MOST accurate is that hidden corrosion is a serious problem with _____ hoops.

   A. the round hoops but not with the flat
   B. the flat hoops but not with the round
   C. both types of
   D. neither type of

29. While on AFID, you come across a clothing factory which shows evidence of poor housekeeping practices.
For you to imply to the owner that the Fire Department will conduct frequent inspections of his premises until satisfactory conditions are maintained is

   A. *proper,* mainly because the owner may be persuaded by it to maintain satisfactory conditions
   B. *improper,* mainly because the owner may feel that he is being harassed
   C. *proper,* mainly because any means which result in the elimination of hazardous conditions are permissible
   D. *improper,* mainly because threats which may not be carried out should not be made

30. Generally, officers on fire prevention inspection duty do not inspect the living quarters of private dwellings unless the occupants agree to the inspection.
The BEST of the following explanations of why private dwellings are excluded from compulsory inspections is that

   A. private dwellings seldom catch fire
   B. fires in private dwellings are more easily extinguished than other types of fires
   C. people may resent such inspections as an invasion of privacy
   D. the monetary value of private dwellings is lower than that of other types of occupancies

KEY (CORRECT ANSWERS)

1.	C	11.	A	21.	A
2.	D	12.	A	22.	B
3.	A	13.	B	23.	B
4.	B	14.	B	24.	A
5.	D	15.	A	25.	C
6.	A	16.	C	26.	A
7.	B	17.	A	27.	D
8.	D	18.	D	28.	B
9.	C	19.	A	29.	A
10.	A	20.	B	30.	C

EXAMINATION SECTION
TEST 1

DIRECTIONS: Each question or incomplete statement is followed by several suggested answers or completions. Select the one that BEST answers the question or completes the statement. *PRINT THE LETTER OF THE CORRECT ANSWER IN THE SPACE AT THE RIGHT.*

1. It is the policy of the department to hold each inspector responsible for formal work assignments given to him.
   Of the following, the BEST reason for this is that it
   A. enables division personnel to keep track of the work schedule
   B. encourages inspectors to be careful with written documents
   C. increases the speed with which inspections are carried out
   D. provides a double check on the time sheet records of inspectors

1.____

2. Assume that you are faced with delays caused by absences of team members due to illness.
   Of the following, the BEST means of handling this problem is to
   A. have your team members keep an accurate record of their absences so that you will be able to identify anyone who is becoming accident-prone
   B. insist on prompt notification at all times when someone on your tea is absent because of illness
   C. require that your team members submit a memorandum informing you of the days on which they will be absent
   D. take over all tasks assigned to your team members when they are absent

2.____

3. Assume that one of the men on your team tells you that he has a problem and would like to discuss it with you privately. During the course of this meeting, it becomes apparent that the man's difficulty stems from conflicts he is having with his wife.
   Of the following, the BEST course of action that you, his supervisor, should take in this situation is to
   A. advise the employee to meet with your superior, who might be able to give him more objective advice
   B. gather enough facts to advise the man about definite solutions for his problem
   C. help the man analyze what the problem is but leave the decision to him
   D. tell the man that you can talk to him only about problems that are job-related

3.____

4. Sometimes it may be advantageous for a senior inspector to let the inspectors under his supervision participate in the development of decisions that must be made about the team's activities.
   The one of the following that is LEAST likely to result when team members participate in supervisory decisions is that the inspectors may

4.____

A. be able to show leadership
B. have a chance to feel creative
C. require closer supervision
D. take more responsibility for minor problems

5. Of the following, the CHIEF reason that the senior inspector should take disciplinary measures as soon as possible after a subordinate inspector's violation of department rules is that
   A. delay will make the senior inspector seem lax
   B. the inspector is more likely to accept the discipline a justified
   C. the supervisor may forget about the offense
   D. there is less likelihood that other inspectors will find out about the offense

6. Assume that you have been directed to institute a new procedure for writing reports about violations encountered during the inspections conducted by the team of which you are in charge. You have heard, through the grapevine, that several of the experienced inspectors on the team have objections to this new procedure.
   Of the following, the BEST course of action for you to take FIRST in this situation is to
   A. issue a written order to put the new procedure into effect
   B. meet with all the inspectors on your team to discuss the procedure
   C. modify the procedure to make it acceptable to all of your inspectors
   D. postpone institution of the new procedure

7. Assume that the head of your unit expects to be out for a week because of illness. You are to act as head of the unit for that time.
   In determining what to do about those inspection duties that you were originally scheduled to perform and which should not be postponed, it would be MOST advisable to
   A. assign them to the inspector who needs training in this area
   B. assign them to the inspector with the most seniority
   C. attempt to do as many of them as possible yourself
   D. divide them among all inspectors who have the time and ability

8. The one of the following situations that is LEAST likely to result from poor planning and organization of an inspection unit's work is that
   A. inspectors will be uncertain about their responsibilities
   B. job performance will be poor
   C. the work will be completed at a steady monotonous pace
   D. there will be a high turnover rate in the unit's staff

9. Of the following, the BEST course of action to take in order to avoid charges of favoritism when making job assignments is to
   A. delegate the authority to make assignments to a well-liked experienced inspector
   B. keep records which may demonstrate proper distribution and rotation of assignments

C. select the oldest inspectors for the most desirable assignments
D. tell the men that, if they have any gripes about their assignments, they should see the supervising inspector

10. Of the following, the MOST important reason for a senior inspector to receive communications from the supervising inspector before they are transmitted to the inspectors is that he can
    A. avoid discussing communications with his subordinates
    B. exercises close supervision over every detail of the inspectors' assignments
    C. limit the amount of information received by his subordinates
    D. maintains his position in the chain of command

11. If an organization has rules that are clear but excessively detailed and rigid, the one of the following which is MOST likely to occur is that
    A. employees will tend to ignore the rules
    B. records of performance will be more difficult to maintain
    C. supervisors will have more difficulty in applying the rules to individual situations
    D. use of individual judgment and discretion will be decreased

12. An effective senior inspector strives to build up the feeling that he and his men are on the same team. The imposition of discipline may serious endanger the relationship built up between him and his men.
    The one of the following steps that the senior inspector may take to insure that the imposition of discipline will NOT cause any deterioration of his relationship with his subordinates is to
    A. avoid disciplinary action, except for very serious offenses
    B. delegate simple disciplinary problems to a competent, experienced inspector
    C. discipline his men in groups so that they will feel as if they were part of a team
    D. impose discipline in as impersonal way as possible

13. Suppose that one of the inspectors under the supervision of a senior inspector is repeatedly late for work. Despite the inspector's habitual lateness, he manages to complete his work assignments on schedule.
    Of the following, the MOST advisable action for the senior inspector to take in this situation is to
    A. ask one of the other inspectors to speak to him about his attendance
    B. ignore the inspector's habitual lateness as long as he does his work properly
    C. reprimand the inspector privately and follow through to see whether his attendance improves
    D. tell him in the presence of the other inspectors that he must improve his attendance record

14. Assume that you are informed by your superior that all reports prepared by your team should be checked by you when possible before their submission to a supervising inspector.
Of the following, the BEST course of action to take if you are too busy to look at all these reports and they have to be sent out right away is to
   A. delegate the responsibility for checking the reports to someone you have carefully instructed in the need for neat and accurate reports
   B. request additional staff from another unit to help you review these reports
   C. send the reports out without checking them and attach an explanatory note, telling your superior that you have not had time to look at them
   D. tell our men to review one another's reports and initial them

15. Assume that a senior inspector notices that another senior inspector divides his team's workload in what seems to him to be an inefficient manner. He decides to report this to the supervising inspector.
Of the following, an accurate evaluation of the action taken by the senior inspector in this situation is that it is GENERALLY
   A. *good* practice, mainly because the supervising inspector is the only person authorized to make this senior inspector divide the work according to standard procedure
   B. *good* practice, mainly because the senior inspector needs close supervision to adequately carry out his responsibilities
   C. *poor* practice, mainly because the senior inspector should have consulted other senior inspectors about this situation
   D. *poor* practice, mainly because the senior inspector should understand that other senior inspectors may manage their operations differently

16. Assume that you have heard a rumor that department rules are about to be changed in a manner which will make certain types of inspections more complicated.
Of the following, the BEST action for you to take in this situation is to
   A. ask the members of your staff, individually, if they have heard such a rumor
   B. call a meeting of your staff to tell them such a change is rumored
   C. make plans to change your unit's procedures to adapt to the new methods
   D. await official confirmation or denial of the rumor

17. Assume that one of the inspectors under your supervision has been doing an excellent job but no longer seems to have any interest in the work. He complains to you that he finds the work boring.
Of the following, the MOST advisable action for you to take FIRST is to
   A. ask some of his fellow inspectors to discuss the matter with him
   B. attempt to vary his assignments and give him more complex assignments
   C. remind him that his evaluation by superiors may depend in part on the interest he shows in his work
   D. suggest that the inspector be transferred to another division

18. The BEST way for you to prepare the inspectors in your unit to handle special assignments speedily and make decisions in an emergency is to
    A. follow each employee's work very carefully so you know where he is least efficient
    B. give them the freedom to make decisions in their everyday work
    C. refuse to accept work that is turned in late
    D. set deadlines ahead of the time when regularly assigned work is actually due so they will learn to work efficiently

18.____

19. Suppose you are supervising several inspectors. One of the inspectors has recently transferred to your unit. You discover that although he generally prepares his reports in a fairly correct way, he does not follow the prescribed procedure that you have taught the other inspectors.
    In this situation, the one of the following that it would be BEST for you to do is to
    A. allow him to use his own procedure if it is accurate and efficient
    B. refer him to your supervisor
    C. discuss the matter with all the inspectors and let them decide which procedure they wish to follow
    D. tell him to follow the procedure used by the other inspectors

19.____

20. Assume that you have one of your most competent inspectors working on a new type of project. As you are reviewing his work, you notice he has made some errors.
    You should
    A. correct the errors yourself, otherwise the inspector will get discouraged
    B. ignore the errors; they are probably not important, especially when the inspector is first learning the job
    C. tell the inspector about the errors; he will probably learn from them
    D. tell the inspector about the errors; then he will be aware that he is careless

20.____

21. Assume that your unit has been given a special assignment to make an original study. You plan to give this assignment to two of your most competent inspectors.
    The BEST way to start them on this work is to
    A. ask the two inspectors how they think the work can be done in a most effective way
    B. do some of the work with the inspectors to make sure they do not make any mistakes
    C. tell the inspectors they will be held directly responsible for the success of the study
    D. write up detailed instructions and give them to the inspectors who will do the work

21.____

6 (#1)

22. Of the following steps in setting up an employee training program, the one which should PRECEDE the others is to
    A. assemble all the materials needed in the training program
    B. decide what training methods would be most effective
    C. determine what facilities are available for training purposes
    D. outline the areas that would be covered in the training program

22.____

23. Assume that you find it necessary to retrain an older, experienced inspector because you are giving this inspector a different kind of assignment.
Of the following, the problem that is MOST likely to arise when retraining such a staff member is that the
    A. instructor will have disciplinary problems with this employee
    B. instructor will know less than this staff member
    C. employee at this status often lacks motivation to be retrained
    D. younger men will be unable to keep up with the performance of this employee

23.____

24. Assume that an inspector has recently been transferred from another unit and is now on your team.
Of the following, the BEST method for you to use to determine whether this man needs any additional instruction or training is to
    A. ask him whether he is having difficulty with the work you assign to him
    B. ask the man's former supervisor whether he was a competent inspector
    C. review the way he handles the various tasks that you assign to him
    D. send this man into the field with one of your inspectors and have him evaluate the newly assigned inspector

24.____

25. Instituting a program of on-the-job training may sometimes present problems for the supervisor because, when first initiated, such training
    A. does not take place under actual working conditions
    B. is less instructive than formal training sessions
    C. may result in a decrease in the authority of the supervisor
    D. may slow down the unit's work

25.____

26. Suppose that you are approached by a newly appointed inspector who asks you to make an inspection visit with him because he is unsure of the procedure.
The one of the following that you should do FIRST is to
    A. agree to make the visit with him
    B. refer him to the supervisor for help
    C. report him to the supervisor for incorrect behavior
    D. tell him to do the best he can and offer to help him write up the report

26.____

27. Suppose that you are writing up your inspection reports in your office on a particular day. A fellow inspector, who has left his identification at home, asks if he may use your identification card and badge in order to perform his scheduled inspections.

27.____

Of the following, you should
- A. allow him to use your identification since he is an inspector
- B. offer to perform the inspections for him if he will write the reports
- C. refuse his request and suggest he explain the situation to the supervisor
- D. tell him you need your identification for yourself

28. Assume that you are assigned to handle telephone complaints. After you have attempted to handle a complaint from a belligerent caller, the caller asks your name, saying that he is going to report you to your superior for being insolent to him.
It would be BEST for you to
- A. give the caller a false name so he will stop bothering you
- B. give the caller your name and explain the circumstances to your superior afterwards
- C. refuse to give the caller your name
- D. tell the caller that you have not been insolent to him

28.____

29. As a senior inspector, you are permitted to hold an outside job as long as it is NOT
- A. dangerous
- B. in conflict with the performance of your inspection duties
- C. mentally or physically taxing
- D. paid at a rate higher than your inspector job

29.____

30. Of the following, the MOST important reason that graphs and charts are used in reports to present material that can be treated statistically is that such material
- A. is easier to understand when it is presented in graph or chart form
- B. looks more impressive when it is presented in graph or chart form
- C. requires less time to prepare when it is presented in a graph or chart form instead of written out
- D. take up less space in graph or chart form than when it is written out

30.____

KEY (CORRECT ANSWERS)

1.	A	11.	D	21.	A
2.	B	12.	D	22.	D
3.	C	13.	C	23.	C
4.	C	14.	A	24.	C
5.	B	15.	D	25.	D
6.	B	16.	D	26.	B
7.	D	17.	B	27.	C
8.	C	18.	B	28.	B
9.	B	19.	D	29.	B
10.	D	20.	C	30.	A

TEST 2

DIRECTIONS: Each question or incomplete statement is followed by several suggested answers or completions. Select the one that BEST answers the question or completes the statement. *PRINT THE LETTER OF THE CORRECT ANSWER IN THE SPACE AT THE RIGHT.*

1. If an inspector finds a discrepancy between the plans and specifications, he should
   A. always follow the plans
   B. ask for an interpretation
   C. always follow the specifications
   D. follow the plans if the difference is in dimensions

   1.____

2. In performing field inspectional work, an inspector is the contact man between the public and the agency, and it is his job to secure compliance through the maximum utilization of persuasion and education and the minimum application of coercion.
   According to this statement, an inspector performing inspectional duties should
   A. seek to obtain voluntary compliance and use coercion only as a last resort
   B. be conciliatory on all issues of non-compliance and not take an attitude of firmness and authority
   C. maintain a strictly impersonal attitude in the exercise of his duties at all times
   D. use the threat of legal action to secure conformance with specified requirements

   2.____

3. The BEST way for a supervising inspector to determine whether a new inspector is learning his work properly is to
   A. ask the other men how this man is making out
   B. question him directly on details of the work
   C. assume that if he asks no questions, he knows the work
   D. inspect and follow up on the work which is assigned to him

   3.____

4. In assigning his men to various jobs, the BEST principle for a supervising inspector to follow is to
   A. study the men's abilities and assign them accordingly
   B. rotate a man from job to job until you find one which he can do well
   C. assign each of them to a job and let them adjust to it in their own way
   D. assume that men appointed to the position can do all parts of the work equally well

   4.____

5. Good inspection methods require that the inspector
   A. be observant and check all details
   B. constantly check with the engineer who designed the job
   C. apply specifications according to his interpretations
   D. permit slight job variation to establish good public relations

   5.____

6. An inspector inspecting a large job under construction inspected plumbing at 9 A.M., heating at 10 A.M., and ventilation at 11 A.M., and did his officework in the afternoon. He followed the same pattern daily for months.
This procedure is
   A. *bad*, because not enough time is devoted to plumbing
   B. *bad*, because the tradesmen know when the inspections will occur
   C. *good*, because it is methodical and he does not miss any of the trades
   D. *good*, because it gives equal amount of time to the important trades

7. The BEST way to evaluate the overall state of completion of a construction project is to check the progress estimate against the
   A. inspection worksheet   B. construction schedule
   C. inspector's checklist   D. equipment maintenance schedule

8. When a contractor fails to adhere to an approved progress schedule, he should
   A. revise the schedule without delay
   B. ask for an extension of time on account of delays
   C. adopt such additional means and methods of construction as will make up for time lost
   D. take no immediate action with the hope that sufficient time will be available later on that will assure the completion in accordance with the schedule

9. The usual contract for agency work includes a section entitled instructions to bidders, which states that the
   A. contractor agrees that he has made his own examination and will make no claim for damages on account of errors or omissions
   B. contractor shall not make claims for damages of any discrepancy, error or omission in any plans
   C. estimates of quantities and calculations are guaranteed by the agency to be correct and are deemed to be a representation of the conditions affecting the work
   D. plans, measurement, dimensions, and conditions under which the work is to be performed are guaranteed by the agency

10. A lump sum type of contract may require the contractor to submit a schedule of unit price.
    The BEST reason for this is that it
    A. prevents the lump sum from being too high
    B. simplifies the selection of the lowest bidder
    C. enables the estimators to check the total cost
    D. provides a means of making equitable partial payments

11. A contractor on a large construction project USUALLY receives partial payments based on
    A. estimates of completed work
    B. actual cost of materials delivered and work completed
    C. estimates of material delivered and not paid for by the contractor
    D. the breakdown estimate submitted after the contract was signed and prorated over the estimated duration of the contract

11.____

12. In order to avoid disputes over payments for extra work in a contract for construction, the BEST procedure to follow would be to
    A. have contractor submit work progress reports daily
    B. insert a special clause in the contract specifications
    C. have a representative on the job at all times to verify conditions
    D. allocate a certain percentage of the cost of the job to cover such expenses

12.____

13. A fixed amount of money is generally withheld from the contractor for a definite period after the completion of construction.
    The BEST reason for this is
    A. that the money will be available for taxes due
    B. to penalize the contractor for poor work
    C. that it is a security for the repair of any defective work
    D. that the money will be available for modifications in the design of the structure

13.____

14. Prior to the installation of equipment called for in the specifications, the contractor is USUALLY required to submit for approval
    A. sets of shop drawings
    B. a set of revised specifications
    C. a detailed description of the methods of work to be used
    D. a complete list of skilled and unskilled tradesmen he proposes to use

14.____

15. During the actual construction work, the CHIEF value of a construction schedule is to
    A. insure that the work will be done on time
    B. reveal whether production is falling behind
    C. show how much equipment and material is required for the project
    D. furnish data as to the methods and techniques of construction operations

15.____

16. Of the following items, the one which should NOT be included in a proposed work schedule is
    A. a schedule of hourly wage rates and supplementary benefits
    B. an estimated time required for delivery of materials and equipment
    C. the anticipated commencement and completion of the various operations
    D. the sequence and inter-relationship of various operations with those of related contracts

16.____

17. The frequency with which job reports are submitted should depend MAINLY on   17._____
    A. how comprehensive the report has to be
    B. the amount of information in the report
    C. the availability of an experienced man to write the report
    D. the importance of changes in the information included in the report

18. The CHIEF purpose in preparing an outline for a report is usually to insure that   18._____
    A. the report will be grammatically correct
    B. every point will be given equal emphasis
    C. principal and secondary points will be properly integrated
    D. the language of the report will be of the same level and include the same technical terms

19. The MAIN reason for requiring written job reports is to   19._____
    A. avoid the necessity of oral orders
    B. develop better methods of doing the work
    C. provide a permanent record of what was done
    D. increase the amount of work that can be done

20. Assume you are recommending in a report to your superior that a radical change in a standard maintenance procedure should be adopted.   20._____
    Of the following, the MOST important information to be included in this report is
    A. a list of the reasons for making this change
    B. the names of others who favor the change
    C. a complete description of the present procedure
    D. amount of training time needed for the new procedure

KEY (CORRECT ANSWERS)

1.	B	11.	A
2.	A	12.	C
3.	B	13.	C
4.	A	14.	A
5.	A	15.	B
6.	B	16.	A
7.	B	17.	D
8.	C	18.	C
9.	A	19.	C
10.	D	20.	A

EXAMINATION SECTION
TEST 1

DIRECTIONS: Each question or incomplete statement is followed by several suggested answers or completions. Select the one that BEST answers the question or completes the statement. *PRINT THE LETTER OF THE CORRECT ANSWER IN THE SPACE AT THE RIGHT.*

1. You are following up on the inspections which have been made by one of your inspectors whose work is usually satisfactory. You visit an establishment recently inspected by him and note several violations of the Code which the inspector had failed to report. You discuss the matter with the inspector who becomes highly indignant and insists that the establishment complied with the provisions of the Code at the time of his inspection.
Under the circumstances, it would be MOST advisable for you to state that
    A. a report of the incident, submitted to the borough chief, will be included in the inspector's personnel file
    B. at the time of your visit the premises did not comply with some of the provisions of the Code
    C. future failure to report violations of the Code will be regarded as presumptive evidence of collusion
    D. you will recommend a transfer or termination of employment of the inspector if the situation occurs again

1.____

2. You have been assigned to spotcheck the daily report of an inspector. The inspector has indicated that he inspected a certain establishment at 3 P.M. The owner of the establishment insists that the inspector inspected the premises at 11 A.M.
Of the following courses of action, you should FIRST
    A. interview the owners of the establishment visited by the inspector before and after the establishment in question
    B. secure the inspector's daily report for the previous day and check every stop on that report
    C. telephone the inspector to determine the actual time of his visit
    D. write a formal memorandum to the borough chief regarding the incident

2.____

3. You are investigating the complaint made by the owner of an establishment who alleged that an inspector spoke to him in a loud and disrespectful manner while inspecting his premises. You interview the complainant and ask him if he has any witnesses to support his complaint. He tells you that he does not. You note that the inspector found several violations of the Code in the course of his inspection of the premises.
Under these circumstances, you should
    A. assure the owner that in the interest of good public relations the inspector involved will not be assigned to inspect the owner's premises in the future
    B. discuss the matter with the inspector before submitting your report

3.____

C. inform the owner that complaints which cannot be substantiated cannot receive further consideration
D. mark the complaint *not substantiated* and refrain from discussing it with the inspector

4. You are assigned to work with another inspector on a complex inspectional problem which has received considerable newspaper publicity. After the field work is completed, you agree to prepare a report incorporating both findings. You prepare the report and submit it directly to your superior without showing it to your fellow inspector. At a staff conference, your superior praises your report and the work performed by you; he minimizes the performance of your fellow inspector. You remain silent. Later you learn that your fellow inspector has been aggrieved by your conduct.
Of the following courses of action, it is MOST advisable that you
   A. ask the inspector whether he wishes you to try to get more credit for him
   B. discuss the matter with your fellow inspector and later with your superior to point out that the inspection was a joint effort and that your colleague should share in the credit
   C. ignore the matter and allow time to take care of the incident
   D. write a memorandum to your superior detailing precisely the work performed by the other inspector in connection with the assignment

4.____

5. Assume that you are a licensed pharmacist and would like to secure a part-time job as a pharmacist to supplement your income. In the course of your work as an inspector, you investigate an anonymous complaint against a drug store. Your investigation discloses nothing to indicate that the drug store owner has violated any provision of the Code. The owner, learning that you are a licensed pharmacist, asks you to work for him on a part-time basis.
Under the circumstances, you SHOULD
   A. *accept*, provided that the owner has not asked you for special consideration
   B. *accept*, provided that you will receive the union scale of wages
   C. *refuse* the offer since a conflict of interest situation may be involved
   D. *refuse* the offer until you have a chance to discuss it with other inspectors who are licensed pharmacists

5.____

6. Your supervisor frequently bypasses you and assigns work directly to your subordinates. You had called this matter to his attention previously. At that time, he assured you that you would not be bypassed again. However, he has continued to bypass you.
Under these circumstances, you SHOULD
   A. attempt to determine the reasons for your supervisor's action before proceeding further
   B. begin keeping a record of the instances when you are bypassed, and forward a memorandum to your supervisor's superior setting forth such instances
   C. ignore the situation until such time as your supervisor brings the matter up for discussion
   D. instruct your staff that they are to accept assignments only from you

6.____

7. In checking the daily reports of one of your inspectors, you notice that he is consistently late in beginning his working day. You discuss the matter with him and point out that disciplinary action may be taken unless he starts work promptly. He denies that he is tardy in beginning his work day. However, based on your field follow-up visits, the evidence indicates that the inspector continues to be late in starting work. Again, you discuss the matter with him and he again denies your contention that he is late in starting work.
You should
   A. again point out the need for starting work promptly and continue checking the inspector's starting time
   B. discuss the matter with other inspectors in the work group to get their advice
   C. ignore the matter as long as the inspector makes about as many inspections as others in the group
   D. report the inspector to your supervisor for appropriate disciplinary action

8. One of the inspectors in your group makes about one-fourth more inspections than any other inspector. However, his inspections do not meet satisfactory standards of quality. After you have given him training in the field, his work improves to a point where it is satisfactory. However, he still makes about one-fourth more inspections than any of the other inspectors.
You should
   A. ask that the inspector be transferred to a unit where the quantity and quality of work produced by him will be closer to the group standard
   B. ask the proprietors of establishments visited by this inspector whether the inspections were too cursory
   C. devote less time to this inspector so that you may devote more time to those inspectors who may need additional training
   D. instruct the inspector to reduce the number of his inspections to the group standard and spend more time in each establishment

9. Assume that your superior has given you an additional job to do which will require extra effort on the part of your inspectors who are now carrying a full work load. You feel that the job cannot be completed in the allotted time. You present your point of view but your superior insists that you handle the assignment without any increase in staff.
Of the following courses of action, it would be MOST advisable for you to
   A. attempt to complete the assignment within the allotted time by rescheduling and re-assigning other work
   B. commit yourself to no specific course of action while attempting to secure evidence to support your position that you should not be given the assignment
   C. insist that your superior give you some assurance that this assignment does not set a precedent for assignments of a similar nature and agree to do the job
   D. take the matter up with higher authority, preferably by memorandum, but apprise your superior of your action

10. You are conducting a conference with the inspectors assigned to you. During the conference, you make a statement regarding field inspections which you are reasonably certain is correct. One of the inspectors tells you in an offensive manner that your statement is incorrect. Some of the inspectors agree with him; others remain silent.
    Under these circumstances, you SHOULD
    A. ask the inspectors who have not made any comments for their opinions and be guided by their remarks
    B. ignore the offensive manner of the speaker and state that since you are certain that you are correct, the group will be guided by your statement
    C. state that while the manner of the speaker is offensive, he is nevertheless probably correct
    D. state that you will ascertain whether your statement is correct and will advise them of it in the near future

10.____

11. Assume that you are in the habit of writing to your supervisor on subjects related to your duties. Your supervisor tells you that you are writing too many memorandums to him.
    Of the following courses of action, it is MOST preferable for you to
    A. instruct your inspectors not to put in writing communications regarding the work of the unit
    B. refrain from communicating in writing with your supervisor
    C. take no notice of your supervisor's statement since the smooth functioning of an organization depends upon written communication
    D. write to your supervisor only when you feel that it is necessary

11.____

12. You are accompanying one of your recently appointed inspectors on a field inspection. His inspections take an unusually long time to complete since he is extremely meticulous.
    In these circumstances, you should FIRST
    A. assure the inspector of your confidence in his ability to perform his job properly after sufficient training before criticizing his work performance
    B. seek the transfer of the inspector to a position in the department which does not require contact with the public
    C. tell the inspector that if he does not bring his work up to standard immediately, you will report him to your supervisor
    D. urge the inspector to seek employment in a field not related to his present work

12.____

13. A rumor has started among the members of our staff to the effect that you will soon be leaving government service to take a position in private industry. You know that the rumor is untrue.
    You SHOULD
    A. ask your staff not to discuss matters among themselves which relate to your own affairs
    B. inform your staff that you do not intend to take a position in private industry
    C. say nothing about the matter to your staff
    D. tell your staff that you refuse to confirm or deny rumors concerning your employment prospects

13.____

14. You request an inspector to do something in a certain manner. The inspector asks you the reason for performing the operation in the manner suggested by you.
    You SHOULD
    A. change the subject of your discussion
    B. explain to the inspector that it is his job to carry out instructions—not to evaluate them
    C. give the inspector the reason for your request
    D. tell the inspector that if he thinks about the matter he will be able to determine the reason himself

15. You are conducting a conference with your staff. One of your inspectors seems completely disinterested in the discussion.
    To get this inspector to participate, you SHOULD
    A. ask the inspector direct questions related to the subject being discussed
    B. determine if there is any subject this inspector would like the group to discuss
    C. ignore the situation until such time as the inspector shows interest
    D. tell the inspector in a polite way to pay strict attention

16. You are conducting a conference with your staff and are having a great deal of difficulty with one of the inspectors who wants to do all of the talking. You have previously spoken privately to this inspector regarding his habit of *hogging the discussion*—to no avail.
    Under the circumstances, you SHOULD
    A. ask the inspector to act as an auditor only during conferences
    B. elicit discussion by direct questioning of other members of the staff
    C. refrain from looking at the inspector when you ask a question; this will make it impossible for him to *get the floor*
    D. tell the inspector to remain silent or to leave the group

17. You telephone one of your inspectors, assigning him to the central office for a period of two days to perform clerical duties. The inspector complains loudly, tells you that he dislikes clerical work and that he is being treated unfairly since there are inspectors in other boroughs who are assigned less frequently to clerical duties. You explain the situation as best you can but the inspector continues to object.
    Under these circumstances, you SHOULD
    A. ask the inspector to disregard the assignment pending your inquiry into practices followed in other boroughs in assigning personnel to clerical duties
    B. promise the inspector that in the future you will do your best to give clerical assignments to people who do not voice objections to such assignments
    C. tell the inspector to report for duty in accordance with your instructions
    D. tell the inspector to take the matter up with your superior

18. In developing an on-the-job training program for inspectors, the FIRST thing which should be determined is
    A. areas in which training is needed
    B. how many inspectors are interested in training
    C. how much will the training program cost
    D. what training aids and facilities are available

19. Assume that a recently appointed and inexperienced inspector is given a difficult assignment. He is not given any specific instructions as to how the assignment should be carried out.
    Such action is
    A. *good*; a new employee needs to be encouraged to exercise his own initiative
    B. *good*; a new employee will remember longer if he learns by himself
    C. *poor*; newly appointed employees usually need guidance
    D. *poor*; the cost of training varies from employee to employee

20. A number of important changes have taken place in several sections of the Code. You are to inform a group of inspectors of these changes and how they are to be implemented. While speaking to the group concerning the changes, one of the inspectors whom you know to be a quick learner complains that you are proceeding too slowly; another inspector whom you know to be the slowest learner in the group tells you that your teaching pace is just right.
    You SHOULD
    A. bring the session to a halt and instruct group members on an individual basis
    B. proceed at a faster rate
    C. proceed at a faster rate but allow more time for breaks
    D. proceed at the same rate

21. As part of a new inspector's training, you observe him as he conducts an inspection. The inspector completes the *score-card* on which he lists certain violations of the Code. You look at the *score-card* and note that although the inspector spoke to the establishment owner about a certain violation, the inspector failed to list the violation on the *score-card*.
    Of the following, the MOST desirable way of pointing out this omission is to
    A. ask the inspector to look at the score-card to see if anything is missing
    B. criticize the inspector in a forthright manner and impress upon him the importance of the probationary period
    C. show the score-card to the owner and ask the owner to indicate the violation which was noted but not recorded
    D. tell the inspector in the presence of the owner to list the violation and make a separate note of the omission for service rating purposes

22. Assume that you are in the field training a recently appointed inspector in inspectional techniques.
    The inspections demonstrated by you SHOULD be of the kind
    A. consistent with the high standards of experienced inspectors

B. performed by the average beginning inspector so as not to unduly discourage the trainee
C. performed by the sanitarian who barely meets the minimum acceptable standard
D. which varies sharply from one inspection to the next so that the new inspector will be able to familiarize himself with various ways in which inspections may be conducted

23. The one of the following which LEAST describes the function of planning at the senior inspector level of supervision is deciding
    A. *how* something should be done
    B. *what* must be done
    C. *who* should do it
    D. *why* something should be done

24. For effective management, delegation of responsibility MUST be accompanied by *appropriate*
    A. authority
    B. commendation
    C. compensation
    D. privilege

25. The one of the following which is LEAST a *staff* function in an organization is
    A. advising
    B. directing
    C. observing
    D. planning

26. Assume that an employee is responsible to two supervisors of equal rank for the proper performance of his duties.
    The principle of good management which is NOT being complied with is
    A. delegation of authority
    B. fixed responsibility
    C. homogeneous assignment
    D. unity of command

27. Where low morale is responsible for low work output, the FIRST step which should be taken is to
    A. determine the reason for the poor state of morale by interviewing supervisors and employees who are directly affected
    B. have the head of the organization deliver an inspirational talk to those responsible for the low work output, stressing the mission of the organization and the importance of the work involved
    C. lower standards of production to equal work output and then gradually increase these standards to the desired level
    D. withdraw privileges with regard to the granting of leave, coffee breaks, and choice of lunch hours until work output rises to a satisfactory level

28. The one of the following which is NOT usually a need which gives rise to a work simplification program in government is the need to
    A. make the job as pleasant as possible for employees
    B. make things more convenient for members of the public
    C. produce a greater quantity and higher quality of work
    D. provide additional employment in times of recession

29. The MOST practical control the inspector has over the contractor when the inspector is not satisfied with the quality of the work is to
    A. discuss withholding payment on that part of the work that is unsatisfactory
    B. threaten to have the contractor thrown off the job
    C. request that the contractor fire the men responsible for the unsatisfactory work
    D. call the owner of the company and explain the situation to him

30. In the absence of a formal training program for inspectors, the BEST of the following ways to train a new man who is to do inspection work is to
    A. give him literature on the subject so that he can learn what he has to know
    B. have him accompany an inspector as the inspector does his work so that he can learn by observing
    C. assign him the job and let him learn on his own
    D. tell him to go to a school at night that specializes in this field so that he will gain the necessary background

KEY (CORRECT ANSWERS)

1.	B	11.	D	21.	A
2.	A	12.	A	22.	A
3.	B	13.	B	23.	D
4.	B	14.	C	24.	A
5.	C	15.	A	25.	B
6.	A	16.	B	26.	D
7.	D	17.	C	27.	A
8.	C	18.	A	28.	D
9.	A	19.	C	29.	A
10.	D	20.	D	30.	B

TEST 2

DIRECTIONS: Each question or incomplete statement is followed by several suggested answers or completions. Select the one that BEST answers the question or completes the statement. *PRINT THE LETTER OF THE CORRECT ANSWER IN THE SPACE AT THE RIGHT.*

1. Assume that you are a supervisor newly assigned to a squad of inspectors. 1.____
   In order to establish a favorable working atmosphere, it is BEST to
   A. discipline ineffective members of your squad at regular intervals
   B. speak extensively on job-related subjects
   C. give advice on personal matters
   D. recognize and accept ideas submitted by members of your squad

2. Assume that you are a supervisor who has in his squad an ambitious inspector 2.____
   studying for promotion. This man takes every opportunity to as you questions
   about your job.
   Under the circumstances, it is BEST for you to
   A. remind him firmly that he already has a full-time job and that if he wishes
      to study for promotion he should do it off-duty by himself
   B. plan your time so that you can assist in his promotional aspirations
   C. tell him that you would like to help but that you do not wish to give him an
      advantage over others
   D. resist instructing him because if he is promoted you will lose a valuable
      man, thereby weakening your squad

3. A signed written complaint has been mailed directly to you alleging that one 3.____
   of your inspectors has been overly aggressive in that he pushed the
   complainant. The inspector is a good worker, and this is the first complaint
   ever recorded against him.
   Under the circumstances, it is BEST to
   A. notify informally the accused inspector of the nature of the complaint, and
      suggest that he guard his behavior in the future
   B. ignore the complaint as being too vague to warrant action
   C. have the complainant carefully investigated to see whether he has made
      similar complaints in the past
   D. have the complaint investigated by someone disinterested in the outcome
      of the matter

4. Assume that you are a supervisor in charge of an inspector who has a good 4.____
   work record but who, for the first time, exhibits symptoms of drunkenness.
   When confronted, he denies that he ever drinks and says that his apparently
   intoxicated behavior is really the result of his doctor's medication for the flu.
   Under the circumstances, it is BEST to
   A. ignore the situation for the present but later report the matter to your
      superiors
   B. tell the man that you know he's untruthful but that, because of his
      previous good record, you are willing to overlook his condition this time

57

C. accept the man's explanation, send him home for the day on sick leave, but watch for future symptoms of possible drunken behavior
D. reprimand the man, send out for coffee to sober him up, and warn him the next time he exhibits drunken symptoms he will face severe disciplinary action

5. Assume that you are in charge of a squad of inspectors. One inspector has been performing ineffectively, although working hard. All attempts to improve his performance have failed. He is nearing the end of his probationary period. In the circumstances, it is BEST to
    A. reschedule assignments so that the rest of the squad takes over a greater share of the work load
    B. recommend separation on the ground that improvement cannot be achieved
    C. assign only the simplest cases to the man
    D. leave the man alone, since he seems to be doing the best he can

6. As a supervisor, you have been instructed by your superiors to install a radically revised system of procedure for your squad. You are concerned that your subordinates may resist the change.
The BEST way for you to secure the willing cooperation of your squad in effecting the change is to
    A. secure the participation of all your subordinates in planning for the change, emphasizing the absence of any threat to their security
    B. *sell* your subordinates on the new procedure by emphasizing that the procedure has the full backing of your superiors
    C. warn your subordinates not to sabotage the change, emphasizing that willful interference with the change will be followed by severe corrective disciplinary action
    D. appeal to your subordinates' loyalty to the agency and to yourself, emphasizing that *one hand washes the other*

7. Supervising inspectors are involved in the decision-making process.
Effective decision-making means MOST NEARLY
    A. compromising, since all decisions involve compromise
    B. selecting the course of action with the least unexpected consequences
    C. holding off on any action until circumstances dictate one particular approach
    D. securing employee participation in the planning and policy process

8. Assume that you are a supervisor in charge of an inspector who may be abusing sick leave.
Under the circumstances, the FIRST thing you should do is to
    A. interview the inspector to find out what is wrong
    B. maintain a calendar of sick leave used by the inspector to see whether a pattern develops indicating abuse
    C. warn the inspector against any further malingering
    D. institute corrective disciplinary action the very next time the inspector reports sick

9. Supervision is a social relationship. It is both the art of being a leader and a subordinate.
   This statement implies that
   A. the supervisory relationship involves an expectation of obedience on the part of the supervisor and a willingness to obey on the part of the subordinate
   B. the really successful supervisor always knows that his subordinates understand him, and doesn't have to clarify and explain his orders
   C. in the supervisory relationship, supervisor and subordinate should strive to be as friendly with each other as possible
   D. the really wise subordinate knows his job and sees to it that his supervisor knows that he knows his job

10. As a supervising inspector, you have a man in your squad who avoids difficult tasks on the ground that he cannot do the more difficult work. You have informally condoned his practice because he is effective and busy on lesser tasks, overall squad production is satisfactory, and no one has complained. Nevertheless, you decide to review the situation.
    Solely on the basis of the information presented, the LEAST effective response to this situation is to
    A. denounce the man before the group and ask for their advice on handling the matter
    B. insist on a basic work capability for all members of the squad
    C. continue the present practice informally, so long as production and morale are unaffected
    D. remind the man that professional recognition awaits those who work hard on a variety of tasks

11. Assume that you are a new supervisor in charge of a squad of inspectors. Your superior informs you that the squad has long been declining in effectiveness. Your job is to increase production without changing personnel.
    Of the following, the MOST important information for you to have in order to effect change is
    A. the reason for the squad's past production successes
    B. an accurate account of your squad's present state of mind
    C. a knowledge of the interplay of psychic needs and neighborhood surroundings in producing the squad's laxity
    D. a case history on every individual so that you can estimate the personal impact of prospective changes

12. Assume that you have become the supervisor of a high morale squad of inspectors, all of whom ae experienced and productive.
    The BEST supervisory approach for you to take to insure the continuance of an efficient squad is to
    A. leave them alone, since it doesn't pay to tinker with a well-running mechanism
    B. develop a close personal relationship with the most experienced member of your squad and use this relationship to govern the rest of the squad

C. take charge immediately, and let them know who's in charge since everything usually runs well when persons are alert
D. work problems out together, on the theory that things usually run well when the supervisor successfully seeks to build power with, rather than hold authority over, his work group

13. One of the things a supervising inspector should AVOID doing is
    A. answering unimportant questions asked by the public
    B. talking to people he does not know
    C. blaming his supervisors for all the unpleasant orders the supervising inspector must issue
    D. showing an interest in public problems

14. An angry building owner complains loudly to you, the supervisor, about the actions of the inspectors assigned to you.
    You should
    A. try to find excuses for your men's actions
    B. speak to him in the same tone of voice he is using
    C. insist that the actions of your men are correct
    D. try to answer his complaint quietly

15. In dealing with the general public, an inspector should remember that
    A. every person is an individual who may think for himself
    B. all people tend to think alike
    C. most people think alike
    D. it is best to change the public's way of thinking to what the department requires

16. An inspector is performing his job in the BEST manner when he
    A. continually checks with his supervisor to make sure each inspection is being done properly
    B. knows enough to overlook minor violations that have a negligible effect on overall
    C. varies the rules when he feels they do not meet the conditions of the job
    D. is careful and observant in his inspections

17. An IMPORTANT characteristic of a good supervisor is his ability to
    A. be a stern disciplinarian   B. put off the settling of grievances
    C. solve problems   D. find fault in individuals

18. At the time you hand out a job assignment, an inspector feels that he cannot complete the job within the time limit you have given him.
    You would expect the inspector FIRST to
    A. make as many inspections as possible and then report to you
    B. compare his workload to that of the other inspectors
    C. complete the work by putting in overtime before notifying you of the problem
    D. request assistance in doing the work

19. A new supervising inspector will BEST obtain the respect of the men assigned to him if he
    A. makes decisions rapidly and sticks to them regardless of whether they are right or wrong
    B. makes decisions rapidly and then changes them just as rapidly if the decisions are wrong
    C. does not make decisions unless he is absolutely sure that they are right
    D. makes his decisions after considering carefully all available information

20. A newly-appointed inspector is operating at a level of performance below that of the other employees.
    In this situation, a supervisor should FIRST
    A. lower the acceptable standard for the new inspector
    B. find out why the new inspector cannot do as well as the others
    C. advise the new inspector he will be dropped from the payroll at the end of the probationary period
    D. assign another new inspector to assist the first inspector

21. Assume that you have to instruct a new inspector on a specific departmental operation. The new man seems unsure of what you have said.
    Of the following, the BEST way for you to determine whether the man has understood you is to
    A. have the man explain the operation to you in his own words
    B. repeat your explanation to him slowly
    C. repeat your explanation to him using simpler wording
    D. emphasize the important parts of the operation to him

22. A supervising inspector realizes that he has taken an instantaneous dislike to a new inspector assigned to him.
    The BEST course of action for this supervisor to take in this case is to
    A. be especially observant of the new inspector's actions
    B. request that the new inspector be reassigned
    C. make a special effort to be fair to the new inspector
    D. ask to be transferred himself

23. A supervisor gives detailed instructions to his inspectors as to how a certain type of job is to be done.
    One ADVANTAGE of this practice is that this will
    A. result in a more flexible operation
    B. standardize operations
    C. encourage new men to learn
    D. encourage initiative in the men

24. Of the following, the one that would MOST likely be the result of poor planning is:
    A. Omissions are discovered after the work is completed.
    B. During the course of normal inspection, a meter is found to be unaccessible.
    C. An inspector completes his assignments for that day ahead of schedule.
    D. A problem arises during an inspection and prevents an inspector from completing his day's assignments.

25. Of the following, the BEST way for a supervisor to maintain good morale among his inspectors is for the supervisor to
    A. avoid correcting an inspector when he makes mistakes
    B. continually praise an inspector's work even when it is of average quality
    C. show that he is willing to assist in solving the inspector's problems
    D. accept the inspector's excuses for failure even though the excuses are not valid

KEY (CORRECT ANSWERS)

1.	D		11.	B
2.	B		12.	D
3.	D		13.	C
4.	C		14.	D
5.	B		15.	A
6.	A		16.	D
7.	B		17.	C
8.	A		18.	D
9.	A		19.	D
10.	A		20.	B

21.	A
22.	C
23.	B
24.	A
25.	C

EXAMINATION SECTION
TEST 1

DIRECTIONS: Each question or incomplete statement is followed by several suggested answers or completions. Select the one that BEST answers the question or completes the statement. *PRINT THE LETTER OF THE CORRECT ANSWER IN THE SPACE AT THE RIGHT.*

1. One of the major objectives of a pre-employment interview is to get the interviewee to respond freely to inquiries.
   The one of the following actions that would be MOST likely to restrict the conversation of the interviewee would be for the investigator to
   A. keep a stenographic record of the interviewee's statements
   B. ask questions requiring complete explanations
   C. pose direct, specific questions to the interviewee
   D. allow the interviewee to respond to questions at his own pace

   1.____

2. One of the reasons for the widespread use of the interview in personnel selection is that the interview
   A. has been shown to be a valid measurement technique
   B. is efficient and reliable
   C. has been demonstrated to result in consistency among raters
   D. allows for flexibility of response

   2.____

3. In conducting a personnel interview, which of the following guidelines would be MOST desirable for the interviewer to follow?
   A. Allocate the same amount of time to each person being interviewed to standardize the process
   B. Ask exactly the same questions of all persons being interviewed to increase the objectivity of the process
   C. Eliminate the use of non-directive techniques because of their subjectivity
   D. Vary his style and technique to fit the purpose of the interview and the people being interviewed

   3.____

4. You are planning to conduct preliminary interviews of applicants for an important position in your department.
   Which of the following planning considerations is LEAST likely to contribute to successful interviews?
   A. Make provisions to conduct interviews in privacy
   B. Schedule your appointments so that interviews will be short
   C. Prepare a list of your objectives
   D. Learn as much as you can about the applicant before the interview

   4.____

5. When dealing with an aggrieved worker, a USEFUL interviewing technique is to
   A. maintain a sympathetic attitude
   B. maintain an attitude of cold impartiality

   5.____

C. assure the subject that you are on his side
D. display a tape recorder to give the subject confidence that no parts of his story will be overlooked

6. The "patterned interview" is a device used by sophisticated employers to
   A. select employees who fit the ethnic pattern of the community
   B. ascertain the pattern of facts surrounding a grievance
   C. discourage workers from joining unions
   D. appraises a subject's most important character traits

7. One of the applicants for a menial job is a tall, stooped, husky individual with a low forehead, narrow eyes, a protruding chin, and a tendency to keep his mouth open.
   In interviewing him, you should
   A. check him more carefully than the other applicants regarding criminal background
   B. disregard any skills he might have for other jobs which are vacant
   C. make your vocabulary somewhat simpler than with the other applicants
   D. make no assumptions regarding his ability on the basis of his appearance

8. Of the following, the BEST approach for you to use at the beginning of an interview with a job applicant is to
   A. caution him to use his time economically and to get to the point
   B. ask him how long he intends to remain on the job if hired
   C. make some pleasant remarks to put him at ease
   D. emphasize the importance of the interview in obtaining the job

9. Of the following, the BEST reason for conducting an "exit interview" with an employee is to
   A. make certain that he returns all identification cards and office keys
   B. find out why he is leaving
   C. provide a useful training device for the exit interviewer
   D. discover if his initial hiring was in error

10. If you are to interview several applicants for jobs and rate them on five different factors on a scale of 1 to 5, you should be MOST careful to *insure* that your
    A. rating on one factor does not influence your rating on another factor
    B. ratings on all factors are interrelated with a minimum of variation
    C. overall evaluation for employment exactly reflects the arithmetic average of your ratings
    D. overall evaluation for employment is unrelated to your individual ratings

11. Of the following, the question MOST appropriate for initial screening purposes GENERALLY is:
    A. What are your salary requirements?
    B. Why do you think you would like this kind of work?
    C. How did you get along with your last supervisor?
    D. What are your vocational goals?

12. Of the following, normally the question MOST appropriate for selection purposes generally would tend to be:
    A. Where did you work last?
    B. When did you graduate from high school?
    C. What was your average in school?
    D. Why did you select this organization?

13. Assume that you have been asked to interview each of several students who have been hired to work part-time.
    Which of the following would ordinarily be accomplished LEAST effectively in such an interview?
    A. Providing information about the organization or institution in which the students will be working
    B. Directing the students to report for work each afternoon at specified times
    C. Determining experience and background of the students so that appropriate assignments can be made
    D. Changing the attitudes of the students toward the importance of parental controls

14. In interviewing job applicants, which of the following usually does NOT have to be done before the end of the interview?
    A. Making a decision to hire an applicant
    B. Securing information from applicants
    C. Giving information to applicants
    D. Establishing a friendly relationship with applicants

15. In the process of interviewing applicants for a position on your staff, the one of the following which would be BEST is to
    A. make sure all applicants are introduced to the other members of your staff prior to the formal interview
    B. make sure the applicant does not ask questions about the job or the department
    C. avoid having the applicant talk with the staff at the conclusion of a successful interview
    D. introduce applicants to some of the staff at the conclusion of a successful interview

16. While interviewing a job applicant, you ask applicant why he left his last job. The applicant does not answer immediately.
    Of the following, the BEST action to take at that point is to
    A. wait until he answers
    B. ask another question
    C. repeat the question in a loud voice
    D. ask him why he does not answer

17. You know that a student applying for a job in your office has done well in college except for two courses in science. However, when you ask him about his grades, his reply is vague and general.

It would be BEST for you to
- A. lead the applicant to admitting doing poorly in science to be sure that the facts are correct
- B. judge the applicant's tact and skill in handling what may be for him a personally sensitive question
- C. immediately confront the applicant with the facts and ask for an explanation
- D. ignore the applicant's response since you have the transcript

18. A college student has applied for a position with your department.
Prior to conducting an interview of the job applicant, it would be LEAST helpful for you to have
- A. a personal resume
- B. a job description
- C. references
- D. hiring requirements

19. Job applicants tend to be nervous during interviews.
Which of the following techniques is MOST likely to put such an applicant at ease?
- A. Try to establish rapport by asking general questions which are easily answered by the applicant
- B. Ask the applicant to describe his career objectives immediately, thus minimizing the anxiety caused by waiting
- C. Start the interview with another member of the staff present so that the applicant does not feel alone
- D. Proceed as rapidly as possible, since the emotional state of the applicant is none of your concern

20. At the first interview between a supervisor and a newly appointed subordinate, GREATEST care should be taken to
- A. build toward a satisfactory personal relationship even if some other objectives of the interview must be postponed
- B. cover a predetermined list of specific objectives so as to make a further orientation interview unnecessary
- C. create an image of a forceful, determined supervisor whose wishes cannot be opposed by a subordinate without great risk
- D. create an impression of efficiency and control of operation free from interpersonal relationships

21. You are a supervisor in an agency and are holding your first interview with a new employee.
In this interview, you should strive MAINLY to
- A. show the new employee that you are an efficient and objective supervisor, with a completely impersonal attitude toward your subordinates
- B. complete the entire orientation process including the giving of detailed job-duty instructions

C. make it clear to the employee that all your decisions are based on your many years of experience
D. lay the groundwork for a good employee-supervisor relationship by gaining the new employee's confidence

22. The INCORRECT statement related to the principles of interviewing is:
    A. Written outlines should be avoided by the interviewer because they tend to be overly restrictive.
    B. Preliminary planning (for the interview) should involve an analysis of the point of view of the person to be interviewed.
    C. An interviewing supervisor should make every effort to conduct it in privacy to avoid possible inhibitions.
    D. Well-planned questions are sometimes necessary in conducting an interview.

23. Assume that you are conducting an interview with a prospective employee who is of limited mental ability and low socio-economic status.
    Of the following, it is MOST likely that asking him many open-ended questions about his work experience would cause him to respond
    A. articulately   B. reluctantly   C. comfortably   D. aggressively

24. An individual interview is to be used as part of an examination for a supervisory position.
    Of the following, the attribute or characteristic that is LEAST suitable for evaluation in such an interview is
    A. ability to supervise people   B. poise and confidence
    C. response to stress conditions   D. rigidity and flexibility

25. In conducting a disciplinary interview, a supervisor finds that he must ask some highly personal questions which are relevant to the problem at hand.
    The interviewer is MOST likely to get TRUTHFUL answers to these questions if he asks them
    A. early in the interview, before the interviewee has had a chance to become emotional
    B. in a manner so that the interviewee can answer them with a simple "yes" or "no"
    C. well into the interview, after rapport and trust have been established
    D. just after the close of the interview, so that the questions appear to be off the record

KEY (CORRECT ANSWERS)

1.	A	11.	A
2.	D	12.	D
3.	D	13.	D
4.	B	14.	A
5.	A	15.	D
6.	D	16.	A
7.	D	17.	B
8.	C	18.	C
9.	B	19.	A
10.	A	20.	A

21.	D
22.	A
23.	B
24.	A
25.	C

TEST 2

DIRECTIONS: Each question or incomplete statement is followed by several suggested answers or completions. Select the one that BEST answers the question or completes the statement. *PRINT THE LETTER OF THE CORRECT ANSWER IN THE SPACE AT THE RIGHT.*

1. Of the following methods of conducting an interview, the BEST is to
   A. ask questions with "yes" or "no" answers
   B. listen carefully and ask only questions that are pertinent
   C. fire questions at the interviewee so that he must answer sincerely and briefly
   D. read standardized questions to the person being interviewed

   1.____

2. An interviewer should begin with topics which are easy to talk about and which are not threatening.
   This procedure is useful MAINLY because it
   A. allows the applicant a little time to get accustomed to the situation and leads to freer communication
   B. distracts the attention of the person being interviewed from the main purpose of the questioning
   C. is the best way for the interviewer to show that he is relaxed and confident on the job
   D. causes the interviewee to feel that the interviewer is apportioning valuable questioning time

   2.____

3. The initial interview will normally be more of a problem to the interviewer than any subsequent interviews he may have with the same person because
   A. the interviewee is likely to be hostile
   B. there is too much to be accomplished in one session
   C. he has less information about the client than he will have later
   D. some information may be forgotten when later making record of this first interview

   3.____

4. Most successful interviews are those in which the interviewer shows a genuine interest in the person he is questioning.
   This attitude would MOST likely cause the individual being interviewed to
   A. feel that the interviewer already knows all the facts in his case
   B. act more naturally and reveal more of his true feelings
   C. request that the interviewer give more attention to his problems, not his personality
   D. react defensively, suppress his negative feelings and conceal the real facts in his case

   4.____

5. When interviewing a person, the interviewer may easily slip into error in rating his subject's personal qualities because of the general impression he receives of the individual.
   This tendency is known as the
   A. "halo" effect   B. subjective bias problem
   C. "person-to-person" error   D. inflation effect

   5.____

6. An interviewer would find an interview checklist LEAST useful for
   A. making sure that all the principal facts are secured in the interview
   B. insuring that the claimant's grievance is settled in his favor
   C. facilitating later research into the nature of the problems handled by the agency
   D. conducting the interview in a logical and orderly fashion

7. There are almost as many techniques of interviewing as there are interviews. Of the following, the LEAST objectionable method is to
   A. ask if interviewee minds being quoted
   B. make occasional notes as important topics some up
   C. take notes unobtrusively
   D. take shorthand notes of every word

8. Questions worded so that the person being interviewed has some hint of the desired answer can modify the person's response.
   The result of the inclusion of such questions in an interview, even when they ae used inadvertently, is to
   A. have no effect on the basic content of the information given by the person interviewed
   B. have value in convincing the person that the suggested plan is the best for him
   C. cause the person to give more meaningful information
   D. reduce the validity of the meaningful information obtained from the person

9. The person MOST likely to be a good interviewer is one who
   A. is able to outguess the person being interviewed
   B. tries to change the attitudes of the persons he interviews
   C. controls the interview by skillfully dominating the conversation
   D. is able to imagine himself in the position of the person being interviewed

10. The "halo effect" is an overall impression on the interviewee, whether favorable or unfavorable, usually created by a single trait. This impression then influences the appraisal of all other factors.
    A "halo effect" is LEAST likely to be created at an interview where the interviewee is a
    A. person of average appearance and ability
    B. rough-looking man who uses abusive language
    C. young attractive woman being interviewed by a man
    D. person who demonstrates an exceptional ability to remember faces

11. Of the following, the BEST way for an interviewer to calm a person who seems to have become emotionally upset as a result of a question asked is for the interviewer to
    A. talk to the person about other things for a short time
    B. ask that the person control himself
    C. probe for the cause of his emotional upset
    D. finish the questioning as quickly as possible

3 (#2)

12. Of the following, the GREATEST pitfall in interviewing is that the result may be affected by the
    A. bias of the interviewee
    B. bias of the interviewer
    C. educational level of the interviewee
    D. educational level of the interviewer

    12._____

13. Assume you are assigned to interview applicants.
    Of the following, which is the BEST attitude for you to take in dealing with applicants?
    A. Assume they will enjoy being interviewed because they believe that you have the power of decision
    B. Expect that they have a history of anti-social behavior in the family, and probe deeply into the social development of family members
    C. Expect that they will try to control the interview, thus you should keep them on the defensive
    D. Assume that they will be polite and cooperative and attempt to secure the information you need in a business-like manner

    13._____

14. A Spanish-speaking applicant may want to bring his bilingual child with him to an interview to act as an interpreter.
    Which of the following would be LEAST likely to affect the value of an interview in which an applicant's child has acted as interpreter?
    A. It may make it undesirable to ask certain questions.
    B. A child may do an inadequate job of interpretation.
    C. A child's answers may indicate his feelings toward his parents.
    D. The applicant may not want to reveal all information in front of his child.

    14._____

15. In answering questions asked by students, faculty, and the public, it is MOST important that
    A. you indicate your source of information
    B. you are not held responsible for the answers
    C. the facts you give be accurate
    D. the answers cover every possible aspect of each question

    15._____

16. Assume that someone you are interviewing is reluctant to give you certain information.
    He would probably be MORE responsive if you show him that
    A. all the other persons you interviewed provided you with the information
    B. it would serve his own best interests to give you the information
    C. the information is very important to you
    D. you are business-like and take a no-nonsense approach

    16._____

17. Taking notes while you are interviewing someone is MOST likely to
    A. arouse doubts as to your trustworthiness
    B. give the interviewee confidence in your ability
    C. insure that you record the facts you think are important
    D. make the responses of the interviewee unreliable

    17._____

18. In developing a role-playing situation to be used to train interviewers, the one of the following that it would be MOST important to use as a guide is that the situation
    A. allow the role player to identify readily with the role he is to play
    B. be free of actual or potential conflict between the role players
    C. can be clearly recognized by the participants as an actual interview situation that has already taken place
    D. should provide a detailed set of specifications for handling the roles to be played

18.____

19. Restating a question before the person being interviewed gives an answer to the original question is usually NOT good practice principally because
    A. the client will think that you don't know your job
    B. it may confuse the client
    C. the interviewer should know exactly what to ask and how to put the question
    D. it reveals the interviewer's insecurity

19.____

20. In interviewing a man who has a grievance, it is IMPORTANT that the interviewer
    A. take note of such physical responses as shifty eyes
    B. use a lie detector, if possible, to ascertain the truth in doubtful situations
    C. allow the complainant to "tell his story"
    D. place the complainant under oath

20.____

21. Ideally, the setting for an interview should NOT include
    A. an informal opening   B. privacy and comfort
    C. an atmosphere of leisure D. a lie detector

21.____

22. Which of the following is an example of a "non-directive" interview?
    A. The subject directs his remarks at someone other than the interviewer.
    B. The subject discusses any topics that seem to be relevant to him.
    C. The subject has not been directed that he need answer any particular questions.
    D. The interview is confined to the facts of the case and is not directed at eliciting personal information.

22.____

23. Of the following abilities, the one which is LEAST important in conducting an interview is the ability to
    A. ask the interviewee pertinent questions
    B. evaluate the interviewee on the basis of appearance
    C. evaluate the responses of the interviewee
    D. gain the cooperation of the interviewee

23.____

24. Which of the following actions would be LEAST desirable for you to take when you have to conduct an interview?
    A. Set a relaxed and friendly atmosphere
    B. Plan your interview ahead of time
    C. Allow the person interviewed to structure the interview as he wishes
    D. Include some stock or standard question which you ask everyone.

25. One of the MOST important techniques for conducting good interviews is
    A. asking the applicant questions in rapid succession, thereby keeping the conversation properly focused
    B. listening carefully to all that the applicant has to say, making mental notes of possible areas for follow-up
    C. indicating to the applicant the criteria and standards on which you will base your judgment
    D. making sure that you are interrupted about five minutes before you wish to end so that you can keep on schedule

KEY (CORRECT ANSWERS)

1.	B	11.	A
2.	A	12.	B
3.	C	13.	D
4.	B	14.	C
5.	A	15.	C
6.	B	16.	B
7.	C	17.	C
8.	D	18.	A
9.	D	19.	B
10.	A	20.	C

21.	D
22.	B
23.	B
24.	C
25.	B

COMMUNICATION
EXAMINATION SECTION
TEST 1

DIRECTIONS: Each question or incomplete statement is followed by several suggested answers or completions. Select the one that BEST answers the question or completes the statement. *PRINT THE LETTER OF THE CORRECT ANSWER IN THE SPACE AT THE RIGHT.*

1. In some agencies the counsel to the agency head is given the right to bypass the chain of command and issue orders directly to the staff concerning matters that involve certain specific processes and practices.
   This situation MOST nearly illustrates the principle of _____ authority.
   A. the acceptance theory of
   B. multiple-linear
   C. splintered
   D. functional

   1.____

2. It is commonly understood that communication is an important part of the administrative process.
   Which of the following is NOT a valid principle of the communication process in administration?
   A. The channels of communication should be spontaneous.
   B. The lines of communication should be as direct and as short as possible.
   C. Communications should be authenticated.
   D. The persons serving in communications centers should be competent.

   2.____

3. Of the following, the one factor which is generally considered LEAST essential to successful committee operations is
   A. stating a clear definition of the authority and scope of the committee
   B. selecting the committee chairman carefully
   C. limiting the size of the committee to four persons
   D. limiting the subject matter to that which can be handled in group discussion

   3.____

4. Of the following, the failure by line managers to accept and appreciate the benefits and limitations of a new program or system VERY FREQUENTLY can be traced to the
   A. budgetary problems involved
   B. resultant need to reduce staff
   C. lack of controls it engenders
   D. failure of top management to support its implementation

   4.____

5. If a manager were thinking about using a committee of subordinates to solve an operating problem, which of the following would generally NOT be an advantage of such use of the committee approach?
   A. Improved coordination
   B. Low cost
   C. Increased motivation
   D. Integrated judgment

   5.____

6. Every supervisor has many occasions to lead a conference or participate in a conference of some sort.
Of the following statements that pertain to conferences and conference leadership, which is generally considered to be MOST valid?
   A. Since World War II, the trend has been toward fewer shared decisions and more conferences.
   B. The most important part of a conference leader's job is to direct discussion.
   C. In providing opportunities for group interaction, management should avoid consideration of its past management philosophy.
   D. A good administrator cannot lead a good conference if he is a poor public speaker.

7. Of the following, it is usually LEAST desirable for a conference leader to
   A. call the name of a person after asking a question
   B. summarize proceedings periodically
   C. make a practice of repeating questions
   D. ask a question without indicating who is to reply

8. Assume that, in a certain organization, a situation has developed in which there is little difference in status or authority between individuals.
Which of the following would be the MOST likely result with regard to communication in this organization?
   A. Both the accuracy and flow of communication will be improved.
   B. Both the accuracy and flow of communication will substantially decrease.
   C. Employees will seek more formal lines of communication.
   D. Neither the flow nor the accuracy of communication will be improved over the former hierarchical structure.

9. The main function of many agency administrative officers is "information management." Information that is received by an administrative officer may be classified as active or passive, depending upon whether or not it requires the recipient to take some action.
Of the following, the item received which is clearly the MOST active information is
   A. an appointment of a new staff member
   B. a payment voucher for a new desk
   C. a press release concerning a past event
   D. the minutes of a staff meeting

10. Of the following, the one LEAST considered to be a communication barrier is
    A. group feedback   B. charged words
    C. selective perception D. symbolic meanings

11. Management studies support the hypothesis that, in spite of the tendency of employees to censor the information communicated to their supervisor, subordinates are more likely to communicate problem-oriented information UPWARD when they have a
    A. long period of service in the organization
    B. high degree of trust in the supervisor
    C. high educational level
    D. low status on the organizational ladder

11.____

12. Electronic data processing equipment can produce more information faster than can be generated by any other means.
    In view of this, the MOST important problem faced by management at present is to
    A. keep computers fully occupied
    B. find enough computer personnel
    C. assimilate and properly evaluate the information
    D. obtain funds to establish appropriate information systems

12.____

13. A well-designed management information system essentially provides each executive and manager the information he needs for
    A. determining computer time requirements
    B. planning and measuring results
    C. drawing a new organization chart
    D. developing a new office layout

13.____

14. It is generally agreed that management policies should be periodically reappraised and restated in accordance with current conditions.
    Of the following, the approach which would be MOST effective in determining whether a policy should be revised is to
    A. conduct interviews with staff members at all levels in order to ascertain the relationship between the policy and actual practice
    B. make proposed revisions in the policy and apply it to current problems
    C. make up hypothetical situations using both the old policy and a revised version in order to make comparisons
    D. call a meeting of top level staff in order to discuss ways of revising the policy

14.____

15. Your superior has asked you to notify division employees of an important change in one of the operating procedures described in the division manual. Every employee presently has a copy of this manual.
    Which of the following is normally the MOST practical way to get the employees to understand such a change?
    A. Notify each employee individually of the change and answer any questions he might have
    B. Send a written notice to key personnel, directing them to inform the people under them

15.____

C. Call a general meeting, distribute a corrected page for the manual, and discuss the change
D. Send a memo to employees describing the change in general terms and asking them to make the necessary corrections in their copies of the manual

16. Assume that the work in your department involves the use of any technical terms.
In such a situation, when you are answering inquiries from the general public, it would usually be BEST to
   A. use simple language and avoid the technical terms
   B. employ the technical terms whenever possible
   C. bandy technical terms freely, but explain each term in parentheses
   D. apologize if you are forced to use a technical term

16.____

17. Suppose that you receive a telephone call from someone identifying himself as an employee in another city department who asks to be given information which your own department regards as confidential.
Which of the following is the BEST way of handling such a request?
   A. Give the information requested, since your caller as official standing
   B. Grant the request, provided the caller gives you a signed receipt
   C. Refuse the request, because you have no way of knowing whether the caller is really who he claims to be
   D. Explain that the information is confidential and inform the caller of the channels he must go through to have the information released to him

17.____

18. Studies show that office employees place high importance on the social and human aspects of the organization. What office employees like best about their jobs is the kind of people with whom they work. So strive hard to group people who are most likely to get along well together.
Based on this information, it is MOST reasonable to assume that office workers are most pleased to work in a group which
   A. is congenial
   B. has high productivity
   C. allows individual creativity
   D. is unlike other groups

18.____

19. A certain supervisor does not compliment members of his staff when they come up with good ideas. He feels that coming up with good ideas is part of the job and does not merit special attention.
This supervisor's practice is
   A. *poor*, because recognition for good ideas is a good motivator
   B. *poor*, because the staff will suspect that the supervisor has no good ideas of his own
   C. *good*, because it is reasonable to assume that employees will tell their supervisor of ways to improve office practice
   D. *good*, because the other members of the staff are not made to seem inferior by comparison

19.____

20. Some employees of a department have sent an anonymous letter containing many complaints to the department head.
    Of the following, what is this MOST likely to show about the department?
    A. It is probably a good place to work.
    B. Communications are probably poor.
    C. The complaints are probably unjustified.
    D. These employees are probably untrustworthy.

21. Which of the following actions would usually be MOST appropriate for a supervisor to take after receiving an instruction sheet from his superior explaining a new procedure which is to be followed?
    A. Put the instruction sheet aside temporarily until he determines what is wrong with the old procedure.
    B. Call his superior and ask whether the procedure is one he must implement immediately.
    C. Write a memorandum to the superior asking for more details.
    D. Try the new procedure and advise the superior of any problems or possible improvements.

22. Of the following, which one is considered the PRIMARY advantage of using a committee to resolved a problem in an organization?
    A. No one person will be held accountable for the decision since a group of people was involved.
    B. People with different backgrounds give attention to the problem.
    C. The decision will take considerable time so there is unlikely to be a decision that will later be regretted.
    D. One person cannot dominate the decision-making process.

23. Employees in a certain office come to their supervisor with all their complaints about the office and the work. Almost every employee has had at least one minor complaint at some time.
    The situation with respect to complaints in this office may BEST be described as probably
    A. *good*; employees who complain care about their jobs and work hard
    B. *good*; grievances brought out into the open can be corrected
    C. *bad*; only serious complaints should be discussed
    D. *bad*; it indicates the staff does not have confidence in the administration

24. The administrator who allows his staff to suggest ways to do their work will usually find that
    A. this practice contributes to high productivity
    B. the administrator's ideas produce greater output
    C. clerical employees suggest inefficient work methods
    D. subordinate employees resent performing a management function

25. The MAIN purpose for a supervisor's questioning the employees at a conference he is holding is to　　　　25.____
    A. stress those areas of information covered but not understood by the participants
    B. encourage participants to think through the problem under discussion
    C. catch those subordinates who are not paying attention
    D. permit the more knowledgeable participants to display their grasp of the problems being discussed

---

KEY (CORRECT ANSWERS)

1.	D		11.	B
2.	A		12.	C
3.	C		13.	B
4.	D		14.	A
5.	B		15.	C
6.	B		16.	A
7.	C		17.	D
8.	D		18.	A
9.	A		19.	A
10.	A		20.	B

21.	D
22.	B
23.	B
24.	A
25.	B

TEST 2

DIRECTIONS: Each question or incomplete statement is followed by several suggested answers or completions. Select the one that BEST answers the question or completes the statement. *PRINT THE LETTER OF THE CORRECT ANSWER IN THE SPACE AT THE RIGHT.*

1. For a superior to use *consultative supervision* with his subordinates effectively, it is ESSENTIAL that he
   A. accept the fact that his formal authority will be weakened by the procedure
   B. admit that he does not know more than all his men together and that his ideas are not always best
   C. utilize a committee system so that the procedure is orderly
   D. make sure that all subordinates are consulted so that no one feels left out

   1.____

2. The *grapevine* is an informal means of communication in an organization. The attitude of a supervisor with respect to the grapevine should be to
   A. ignore it since it deals mainly with rumors and sensational information
   B. regard it as a serious danger which should be eliminated
   C. accept it as a real line of communication which should be listened to
   D. utilize it for most purposes instead of the official line of communication

   2.____

3. The supervisor of an office that must deal with the public should realize that planning in this type of work situation
   A. is useless because he does not know how many people will request service or what service they will request
   B. must be done at a higher level but that he should be ready to implement the results of such planning
   C. is useful primarily for those activities that are not concerned with public contact
   D. is useful for all the activities of the office, including those that relate to public contact

   3.____

4. Assume that it is your job to receive incoming telephone calls. Those calls which you cannot handle yourself have to be transferred to the appropriate office.
   If you receive an outside call for an extension line which is busy, the one of the following which you should do FIRST is to
   A. interrupt the person speaking on the extension and tell him a call is waiting
   B. tell the caller the line is busy and let him know every thirty seconds whether or not it is free
   C. leave the caller on "hold" until the extension is free
   D. tell the caller the line is busy and ask him if he wishes to wait

   4.____

5. Your superior has subscribed to several publications directly related to your division's work, and he has asked you to see to it that the publications are circulated among the supervisory personnel in the division. There are eight supervisors involved.
The BEST method of insuring that all eight see these publications is to
   A. place the publication in the division's general reference library as soon as it arrives
   B. inform each supervisor whenever a publication arrives and remind all of them that they are responsible for reading it
   C. prepare a standard slip that can be stapled to each publication, listing the eight supervisors and saying, "Please read, initial your name, and pass along"
   D. send a memo to the eight supervisors saying that they may wish to purchase individual subscriptions in their own names if they are interested in seeing each issue

5.____

6. Your superior has telephoned a number of key officials in your agency to ask whether they can meet at a certain time next month. He has found that they can all make it, and he has asked you to confirm the meeting.
Which of the following is the BEST way to confirm such a meeting?
   A. Note the meeting on your superior's calendar.
   B. Post a notice of the meeting on the agency bulletin board.
   C. Call the officials on the day of the meeting to remind them of the meeting.
   D. Write a memo to each official involved, repeating the time and place of the meeting.

6.____

7. Assume that a new city regulation requires that certain kinds of private organizations file information forms with your department. You have been asked to write the short explanatory message that will be printed on the front cover of the pamphlet containing the forms and instructions.
Which of the following would be the MOST appropriate way of beginning this message?
   A. Get the readers' attention by emphasizing immediately that there are legal penalties for organizations that fail to file before a certain date.
   B. Briefly state the nature of the enclosed forms and the types of organizations that must file.
   C. Say that your department is very sorry to have to put organizations to such an inconvenience.
   D. Quote the entire regulation adopted by the city, even if it is quite long and is expressed din complicated legal language.

7.____

8. Suppose that you have been told to make up the vacation schedule for the 18 employees in a particular unit. In order for the unit to operate effectively, only a few employees can be on vacation at the same time.
Which of the following is the MOST advisable approach in making up the schedule?
   A. Draw up a schedule assigning vacations in alphabetical order
   B. Find out when the supervisors want to take their vacations, and randomly assign whatever periods are left to the non-supervisory personnel

8.____

C. Assign the most desirable times to employees of longest standing and the least desirable times to the newest employees
D. Have all employees state their own preference, and then work out any conflicts in consultation with the people involved

9. Assume that you have been asked to prepare job descriptions for various positions in your department.
Which of the following are the basic points that should be covered in a *job description*?
   A. General duties and responsibilities of the position, with examples of day-to-day tasks
   B. Comments on the performances of present employees
   C. Estimates of the number of openings that may be available in each category during the coming year
   D. Instructions for carrying out the specific tasks assigned to your department

9._____

10. Of the following, the biggest DISADVANTAGE in allowing a free flow of communications in an agency is that such a free flow
    A. decreases creativity
    B. increases the use of the *grapevine*
    C. lengthens the chain of command
    D. reduces the executive's power to direct the flow of information

10._____

11. A downward flow of authority in an organization is one example of _____ communication.
    A. horizontal   B. informal   C. circular   D. vertical

11._____

12. Of the following, the one that would MOST likely block effective communication is
    A. concentration only on the issues at hand
    B. lack of interest or commitment
    C. use of written reports
    D. use of charts and graphs

12._____

13. An ADVANTAGE of the *lecture* as a teaching tool is that it
    A. enables a person to present his ideas to a large number of people
    B. allows the audience to retain a maximum of the information given
    C. holds the attention of the audience for the longest time
    D. enables the audience member to easily recall the main points

13._____

14. An ADVANTAGE of the *small-group* discussion as a teaching tool is that
    A. it always focuses attention on one person as the leader
    B. it places collective responsibility on the group as a whole
    C. its members gain experience by summarizing the ideas of others
    D. each member of the group acts as a member of a team

14._____

15. The one of the following that is an ADVANTAGE of a *large-group* discussion, when compared to a small-group discussion, is that the large-group discussion
    A. moves along more quickly than a small-group discussion
    B. allows its participants to feel more at ease, and speak out more freely
    C. gives the whole group a chance to exchange ideas on a certain subject at the same occasion
    D. allows its members to feel a greater sense of personal responsibility

15.____

KEY (CORRECT ANSWERS)

1.	D	6.	D	11.	D
2.	C	7.	B	12.	B
3.	D	8.	D	13.	A
4.	D	9.	A	14.	D
5.	C	10.	D	15.	C

EXAMINATION SECTION
TEST 1

DIRECTIONS: Each question or incomplete statement is followed by several suggested answers or completions. Select the one that BEST answers the question or completes the statement. *PRINT THE LETTER OF THE CORRECT ANSWER IN THE SPACE AT THE RIGHT.*

1. Managing conflict effectively by avoiding no-win situations, positively influencing the actions of others and using _____ strategies are what make a great leader.
   A. persuasive   B. ambiguous   C. prosecution   D. performance

2. In today's business world, collaboration will bring together people from distinct backgrounds. These collaborative groups may not share common norms, morals or _____, but they can offer unique _____.
   A. vocabulary; perspectives
   B. salaries; vocabulary
   C. modifications; insights
   D. perspectives; salaries

3. E-mail is a great tool for communication; however, which of the following should you be careful of when in electronic communication with a colleague?
   A. Font size
   B. E-mail length
   C. Font color
   D. Tone of voice

4. A formal relationship can BEST be described as
   A. regulated by procedures or directives
   B. personal and relaxed
   C. emotionally distant and very uncomfortable
   D. confusing and unproductive

5. John is in a meeting with his supervisor ad coworkers. He is thinking about what he's going to have for dinner that night when his boss asks him a question. John can repeat back what his supervisor said, but he cannot retain what was said during the meeting.
   This is a classic example of failing to
   A. focus at work
   B. effectively listen
   C. leave personal plans outside the workplace
   D. care about meetings

6. A person's choice of _____ can directly affect communication.
   A. clothing   B. food   C. hygiene   D. words

7. Why is it important to relax when communicating with team members?
   A. Relaxing always means having better ideas.
   B. People will automatically like you more if you are relaxed.

C. If you are nervous, you may talk too quickly and make it hard for others to understand your message or directive.
D. No one likes someone who is always working, so it is important to relax and not work too hard.

8. In order to show you are genuinely interested in what others have to say, you should
   A. tell them how nice they are
   B. repeat what they say back to them
   C. nod and find something to compliment them about
   D. ask questions and seek clarification from them

8.____

9. Jack and James are always arguing with one another. Their supervisor calls each one in separately to talk to them. He asks Jack to think about things from James' point of view and he asks James to do the same for Jack.
What is the supervisor trying to get each person to do?
   A. Get along   B. Be positive
   C. Communicate effectively D. Empathize

9.____

10. When working in groups, disagreements
    A. should be avoided at all costs
    B. are often a healthy way of building understanding and camaraderie
    C. lead coworkers to hate one another and the company they work for
    D. don't happen if the supervisor chooses the right people to work together

10.____

11. If things go wrong in a group situation, it is important to AVOID
    A. the boss   B. disagreements or arguments
    C. scapegoating   D. being polite and fair to one another

11.____

12. If you are a listener who likes to hear the rationale behind a message, your listening style would be described as _____ style.
    A. results   B. process   C. reasons   D. eye contact

12.____

13. Which of the following BEST describes a psychological barrier in communication?
    A. Molly is so stressed about her paying for her mortgage that she can't focus at work right now.
    B. John doesn't understand a lot of the terms the IT specialist used in an e-mail sent out to everyone.
    C. Jerry is a little older and has a hard time hearing everything so sometimes he misses parts of a conversation.
    D. Linda doesn't want to be at the company for longer than a few months, so she doesn't really try too hard to fit in.

13.____

14. Body language, also known as _____, is really important when building rapport with coworkers and communicating effectively.
    A. verbal language   B. kinesthetic
    C. non-verbal communication D. facial expressions

14.____

15. Which of the following might be a good example of someone who has a "closed" posture?
    A. Hands are apart on the arms of the chair.
    B. His/her arms are folded.
    C. They are directly facing you.
    D. They barely speak above a whisper.

16. Which of the following can eye contact be used for?
    A. To give and receive feedback
    B. To let someone know when it is their turn to speak
    C. To communicate how you feel about someone
    D. All of the above

17. Which of the following is NOT a form of non-verbal communication?
    A. Crossing your arms when talking to someone
    B. Using space within the room in a conversation
    C. Clearing your throat before you speak]
    D. Saying "10-4" when asked if you understand

18. Your best friend has just been hired at the company you work for. You notice he has come into work on several occasions after staying out late the night before. His work has not suffered yet, but you fear it will.
    Which of the following actions should you take to help prevent future problems?
    A. Do nothing; he's your friend but it is his life
    B. Try to talk to him and help him see the importance of not creating bad habits.
    C. Talk to your supervisor and tell him your friend isn't suitable for the job
    D. Tell your friend to change his ways or to quit

19. Interacting with coworkers can be positively or negatively affected by _____ when someone's previous biases and assumptions shape their reactions in future situations.
    A. racism   B. past experience
    C. interpersonal skills   D. active listening

20. Which of the following scenarios BEST describes a person who is being subjective?
    A. Sally is fair and honest when she listens to coworkers. She does not take sides and wants the best solution to the problem.
    B. Mike doesn't like Steve, because he thinks Steve is only out for himself. Still, Steve offers valuable insights, so Mike tries not to let personal feelings get in the way of working together.
    C. Jamie is dating Veronica's ex and Veronica just found out. Now, Veronica immediately shoots down anything Jamie suggests during a meeting as irrational and superfluous.
    D. None of the above

21. Which important communications tem is MOST closely defined as "the quality of a sound governed by the rate of vibrations producing it; the degree of highness or lowness of a tone"?
    A. Tone
    B. Pitch
    C. Effective communication
    D. Rationalization

    21.____

22. _____ is when a person tries to make an imprudent and reckless action seem reasonable.
    A. Projection
    B. Self-deception
    C. Past experience
    D. Rationalization

    22.____

23. When holding conversations with coworkers, you should
    A. do most of the talking
    B. let others do most of the talking
    C. try to split time between talking and listening
    D. zone out and wait for the meeting to finish

    23.____

24. A new hire just arrived and you are meeting her for the first time. Which of the following actions is MOST appropriate?
    A. Walk up and introduce yourself with a smile and a handshake
    B. Wait for her to come and introduce herself
    C. Approach her and offer a hug to make her feel welcome
    D. Ignore the new hire; she is likely your competition

    24.____

25. If you are the type of listener who likes to discuss concepts or issues in detail, you would MOST likely fall under which listening style?
    A. Process
    B. Reasons
    C. Results
    D. None of the above

    25.____

KEY (CORRECT ANSWERS)

1.	A	11.	C
2.	A	12.	C
3.	D	13.	A
4.	A	14.	C
5.	B	15.	B
6.	D	16.	D
7.	C	17.	D
8.	D	18.	B
9.	D	19.	B
10.	B	20.	C

21. B
22. D
23. C
24. A
25. A

TEST 2

DIRECTIONS: Each question or incomplete statement is followed by several suggested answers or completions. Select the one that BEST answers the question or completes the statement. *PRINT THE LETTER OF THE CORRECT ANSWER IN THE SPACE AT THE RIGHT.*

1. Which of the following is an example of the BEST practice when communicating in the workplace?
   A. You are horrible with remembering names so you try to use nicknames to cover up for your poor memory.
   B. You only pay attention to the names of people who you work for or who you deem to be "important."
   C. You try to remember everyone's names and use them whenever possible.
   D. None of the above

   1.____

2. Words of civility such as "please" and "thank you" should be used _____ when conversing with coworkers and business partners.
   A. always   B. sometimes   C. rarely   D. never

   2.____

3. When communicating with others, one should _____ stand as close to them as possible and make body contact in order to get an important point across.
   A. always   B. sometimes   C. rarely   D. never

   3.____

4. The MOST appropriate way to end a conversation is to
   A. seek a mutual resolution, but leave abruptly if it continues
   B. find a way to wrap up the conversation so the other person knows it is time to move on
   C. look impatient so hopefully the person will get the hint
   D. tell the other person the conversation should end

   4.____

5. Another name for interpersonal communication in an office setting is
   A. peer-to-peer communication   B. mass communication
   C. virtual reality   D. e-mailing

   5.____

6. Of the following statements, choose the one you feel is the MOST correct.
   A. Devoid of interpersonal communication, people become sick.
   B. Communication is not completely needed for humans.
   C. People are the only animals that need to have relationships in order to survive.
   D. Important communication is not really relevant until after you become an adult.

   6.____

7. John is giving a presentation on ways to communicate effectively with peers. He is having trouble deciding on what to say in his speech.
   Which of the following statements should he AVOID using?
   A. Always try to understand another person's point of view or perspective
   B. Try to imagine what someone is going to say before they actually say it

   7.____

C. Be aware of how non-verbal cues like eye contact and body language affect how your message is received
D. Both B and C

8. Which of the following would MOST affect our perception of communication with coworkers?
   A. Past experiences
   B. Marital problems
   C. Rumors spread about coworkers
   D. None of the above

9. Many people think of communication as both _____ and _____ messages.
   A. formal; informal
   B. hearing; listening
   C. sending; receiving
   D. finding; decoding

10. Why is context important in communication?
    A. It's important to know which buttons to push in order to get what you want.
    B. Saying something to one person may not have the same effect as saying it to someone else.
    C. Context is only important if you are worried about what others think.
    D. None of the above

11. If your brother is normally bright and talkative during the summer, but you notice he gets quiet and subdued in the winter, the MOST likely communication context he is dealing with would be
    A. relational   B. cultural   C. inner   D. physical

12. _____ is an example of a negative nonverbal action you can take.
    A. Smiling
    B. Using a tone of voice that matches your message
    C. Maintaining eye contact
    D. Slumping your shoulders

13. Cultural context can BEST be described as
    A. what people think of as it relates to the event they are participating in (i.e., wedding versus a funeral)
    B. the connection between a father and his son
    C. rules and patterns of Americans versus the Japanese
    D. thoughts, feelings, and sensations inside a person's head

14. Which of the following BEST describes feedback?
    A. Staring at the speaker while he talks
    B. Nodding and smiling while listening to a speaker
    C. Standing an appropriate distance away so the speaker does not get uncomfortable
    D. Trying to speak while the other person is speaking because you have something more important to say

15. Being able to communicate more effectively can be improved upon by
    A. continually making an effort to be as flexible as possible when talking to others
    B. committing to one style of speaking until you master it
    C. using the same style of correspondence as the person with whom you are speaking
    D. always using the opposite style of communication from the person you are speaking to

16. John walks up to Sally and compliments her on the dress she wore to work today. In his mind, John was just being friendly, but Sally went to her manager and filed a harassment charge against John.
    This miscommunication could MOST easily be classified as an error in what?
    A. Reality   B. Perception   C. Friendship   D. Loyalty

17. If a speaker's tone is flat and monotone, which of the following is the MOST likely reaction that listeners will have?
    They will
    A. enthused by the message
    B. enjoy the message but not be overly excited about it
    C. be polite and interested but will not seem very engaged
    D. be bored and uninterested in the message

18. When Steve speaks to his group about his ideas, he generally has a higher pitch to his voice and gesticulates frequently.
    This lead his team members to believe that Steve
    A. is enthusiastic and has great ideas for the group
    B. has had too much caffeine and needs to relax
    C. is trying to show off for the boss and make them look bad
    D. is extremely smart and great at his job

19. _____ is used when a person wants to add stress to key words in communication. It lets the audience understand the mood or feelings of particular words or phrases.
    A. Anger   B. Tone   C. Perception   D. Inflection

20. If Barry tells Bill that his haircut looks "great" and Bill can tell Barry is being insincere, which of the following tones is Barry MOST likely using?
    A. Affectionate   B. Apologetic   C. Threatening   D. Sarcastic

21. As a supervisor, it is important that everyone clearly comprehends everything you communicate to them.
    In order to ensure this happens, which of the following things should you avoid?
    A. Overusing jargon
    B. Explaining something more than once
    C. Speaking slowly and annunciating everything
    D. Having meetings in the morning

22. If your supervisor is looking down at the ground or has his back to you as he is speaking, it MOST clearly indicates to those who are listening to him that the supervisor
    A. is shy and doesn't like speaking in front of people
    B. is disinterested and doesn't care what he's talking about
    C. is approachable and friendly
    D. dislikes his job and wants to get out as soon as possible

23. Interpersonal communication helps you
    A. know what others are thinking
    B. turn into an inspiring speaker, especially in public
    C. learn about yourself
    D. communicate with the general public

24. In general, people who smile more are perceived as
    A. devious
    B. friendly
    C. attractive
    D. easy to manipulate

25. If your supervisor constantly takes advantage of you and expresses his or her opinion often at the expense of you or other workers, which communication style are they MOST likely using?
    A. Nonassertive   B. Assertive   C. Aggressive   D. Peacemaking

KEY (CORRECT ANSWERS)

1.	C		11.	D
2.	A		12.	D
3.	D		13.	C
4.	B		14.	B
5.	A		15.	A
6.	A		16.	B
7.	B		17.	D
8.	A		18.	A
9.	C		19.	D
10.	B		20.	D

21. A
22. B
23. D
24. B
25. C

PREPARING WRITTEN MATERIAL
EXAMINATION SECTION
TEST 1

DIRECTIONS: Each of the sentences in this test may be classified under one of the following four categories:
- A. Faulty because of incorrect grammar or word usage
- B. Faulty because of incorrect punctuation
- C. Faulty because of incorrect capitalization or incorrect spelling
- D. Correct

Examine each sentence carefully to determine under which of the above four options it is best classified. Then, in the space to the right, print the capital letter preceding the option which is the BEST of the four suggested above. (Note that each faulty sentence contains but one type of error. Consider a sentence to be correct if it contains none of the types of errors mentioned, even though there may be other correct ways of expressing the same thought.)

1. He sent the notice to the clerk who you hired yesterday.   1._____
2. It must be admitted, however that you were not informed of this change.   2._____
3. Only the employee who have served in this grade for at least two years are eligible for promotion.   3._____
4. The work was divided equally between she and Mary.   4._____
5. He thought that you were not available at that time.   5._____
6. When the messenger returns; please give him this package.   6._____
7. The new secretary prepared, typed, addressed, and delivered, the notices.   7._____
8. Walking into the room, his desk can be seen at the rear.   8._____
9. Although John has worked here longer than She, he produces a smaller amount of work.   9._____
10. She said she could of typed this report yesterday.   10._____
11. Neither one of these procedures are adequate for the efficient performance of this task.   11._____
12. The typewriter is the tool of the typist; the cash register, the tool of the cashier.   12._____

13. "The assignment must be completed as soon as possible" said the supervisor.   13._____

14. As you know, office handbooks are issued to all new Employees.   14._____

15. Writing a speech is sometimes easier than to deliver it before an audience.   15._____

16. Mr. Brown our accountant, will audit the accounts next week.   16._____

17. Give the assignment to whomever is able to do it most efficiently.   17._____

18. The supervisor expected either your or I to file these reports.   18._____

KEY (CORRECT ANSWERS)

1.	A	11.	A
2.	B	12.	C
3.	D	13.	B
4.	A	14.	C
5.	D	15.	A
6.	B	16.	B
7.	B	17.	A
8.	A	18.	A
9.	C		
10.	A		

TEST 2

DIRECTIONS: Each of the sentences in this test may be classified under one of the following four categories:
- A. Faulty because of incorrect grammar or word usage
- B. Faulty because of incorrect punctuation
- C. Faulty because of incorrect capitalization or incorrect spelling
- D. Correct

Examine each sentence carefully to determine under which of the above four options it is best classified. Then, in the space to the right, print the capital letter preceding the option which is the BEST of the four suggested above. (Note that each faulty sentence contains but one type of error. Consider a sentence to be correct if it contains none of the types of errors mentioned, even though there may be other correct ways of expressing the same thought.)

1. The fire apparently started in the storeroom, which is usually locked.   1.____
2. On approaching the victim, two bruises were noticed by this officer.   2.____
3. The officer, who was there examined the report with great care.   3.____
4. Each employee in the office had a seperate desk.   4.____
5. All employees including members of the clerical staff, were invited to the lecture.   5.____
6. The suggested Procedure is similar to the one now in use.   6.____
7. No one was more pleased with the new procedure than the chauffeur.   7.____
8. He tried to persaude her to change the procedure.   8.____
9. The total of the expenses charged to petty cash were high.   9.____
10. An understanding between him and I was finally reached.   10.____

KEY (CORRECT ANSWERS)

1. D   6. C
2. A   7. D
3. B   8. C
4. C   9. A
5. B   10. A

TEST 3

DIRECTIONS: Each of the sentences in this test may be classified under one of the following four categories:
  A. Faulty because of incorrect grammar or word usage
  B. Faulty because of incorrect punctuation
  C. Faulty because of incorrect capitalization or incorrect spelling
  D. Correct

Examine each sentence carefully to determine under which of the above four options it is best classified. Then, in the space to the right, print the capital letter preceding the option which is the BEST of the four suggested above. (Note that each faulty sentence contains but one type of error. Consider a sentence to be correct if it contains none of the types of errors mentioned, even though there may be other correct ways of expressing the same thought.)

1. They told both he and I that the prisoner had escaped. 1.____

2. Any superior officer, who, disregards the just complaint of his subordinates, is remiss in the performance of his duty. 2.____

3. Only those members of the national organization who resided in the Middle West attended the conference in Chicago. 3.____

4. We told him to give the national organization assignment to whoever was available. 4.____

5. Please do not disappoint and embarass us by not appearing in court. 5.____

6. Although the office's speech proved to be entertaining, the topic was not relevent to the main theme of the conference. 6.____

7. In February all new officers attended a training course in which they were learned in their principal duties and the fundamental operating procedure of the department. 7.____

8. I personally seen inmate Jones threaten inmates Smith and Green with bodily harm if they refused to participate in the plot. 8.____

9. To the layman, who on a chance visit to the prison observes everything functioning smoothly, the maintenance of prison discipline may seem to be a relatively easily realizable objective. 9.____

10. The prisoners in cell block fourty were forbidden to sit on the cell cots during the recreation hour. 10.____

KEY (CORRECT ANSWERS)

1.	A	6.	C
2.	B	7.	A
3.	C	8.	A
4.	D	9.	D
5.	C	10.	C

TEST 4

DIRECTIONS: Each of the sentences in this test may be classified under one of the following four categories:
- A. Faulty because of incorrect grammar or word usage
- B. Faulty because of incorrect punctuation
- C. Faulty because of incorrect capitalization or incorrect spelling
- D. Correct

Examine each sentence carefully to determine under which of the above four options it is best classified. Then, in the space to the right, print the capital letter preceding the option which is the BEST of the four suggested above. (Note that each faulty sentence contains but one type of error. Consider a sentence to be correct if it contains none of the types of errors mentioned, even though there may be other correct ways of expressing the same thought.)

1. I cannot encourage you any. 1._____
2. You always look well in those sort of clothes. 2._____
3. Shall we go to the park? 3._____
4. The man whome he introduced was Mr. Carey. 4._____
5. She saw the letter laying here this morning. 5._____
6. It should rain before the Afternoon is over. 6._____
7. They have already went home. 7._____
8. That Jackson will be elected is evident. 8._____
9. He does not hardly approve of us. 9._____
10. It was he, who won the prize. 10._____

KEY (CORRECT ANSWERS)

1.	A	6.	C
2.	A	7.	A
3.	D	8.	D
4.	C	9.	A
5.	A	10.	B

TEST 5

DIRECTIONS: Each of the sentences in this test may be classified under one of the following four categories:
- A. Faulty because of incorrect grammar or word usage
- B. Faulty because of incorrect punctuation
- C. Faulty because of incorrect capitalization or incorrect spelling
- D. Correct

Examine each sentence carefully to determine under which of the above four options it is best classified. Then, in the space to the right, print the capital letter preceding the option which is the BEST of the four suggested above. (Note that each faulty sentence contains but one type of error. Consider a sentence to be correct if it contains none of the types of errors mentioned, even though there may be other correct ways of expressing the same thought.)

1. Shall we go to the park. 1._____
2. They are, alike, in this particular way. 2._____
3. They gave the poor man sume food when he knocked on the door. 3._____
4. I regret the loss caused by the error. 4._____
5. The students' will have a new teacher. 5._____
6. They sweared to bring out all the facts. 6._____
7. He decided to open a branch store on 33rd street. 7._____
8. His speed is equal and more than that of a racehorse. 8._____
9. He felt very warm on that Summer day. 9._____
10. He was assisted by his friend, who lives in the next house. 10._____

KEY (CORRECT ANSWERS)

1.	B	6.	A
2.	B	7.	C
3.	C	8.	A
4.	D	9.	C
5.	B	10.	D

TEST 6

DIRECTIONS: Each of the sentences in this test may be classified under one of the following four categories:
  A. Faulty because of incorrect grammar or word usage
  B. Faulty because of incorrect punctuation
  C. Faulty because of incorrect capitalization or incorrect spelling
  D. Correct

Examine each sentence carefully to determine under which of the above four options it is best classified. Then, in the space to the right, print the capital letter preceding the option which is the BEST of the four suggested above. (Note that each faulty sentence contains but one type of error. Consider a sentence to be correct if it contains none of the types of errors mentioned, even though there may be other correct ways of expressing the same thought.)

1. The climate of New York is colder than California. 1._____
2. I shall wait for you on the corner. 2._____
3. Did we see the boy who, we think, is the leader. 3._____
4. Being a modest person, John seldom talks about his invention. 4._____
5. The gang is called the smith street bos. 5._____
6. He seen the man break into the store. 6._____
7. We expected to lay still there for quite a while. 7._____
8. He is considered to be the Leader of his organization. 8._____
9. Although I recieved an invitation, I won't go. 9._____
10. The letter must be here some place. 10._____

KEY (CORRECT ANSWERS)

1. A   6. A
2. D   7. A
3. B   8. C
4. D   9. C
5. C   10. A

TEST 7

DIRECTIONS: Each of the sentences in this test may be classified under one of the following four categories:
- A. Faulty because of incorrect grammar or word usage
- B. Faulty because of incorrect punctuation
- C. Faulty because of incorrect capitalization or incorrect spelling
- D. Correct

Examine each sentence carefully to determine under which of the above four options it is best classified. Then, in the space to the right, print the capital letter preceding the option which is the BEST of the four suggested above. (Note that each faulty sentence contains but one type of error. Consider a sentence to be correct if it contains none of the types of errors mentioned, even though there may be other correct ways of expressing the same thought.)

1. I though it to be he. 1.____
2. We expect to remain here for a long time. 2.____
3. The committee was agreed. 3.____
4. Two-thirds of the building are finished. 4.____
5. The water was froze. 5.____
6. Everyone of the salesmen must supply their own car. 6.____
7. Who is the author of Gone With the Wind? 7.____
8. He marched on and declaring that he would never surrender. 8.____
9. Who shall I say called? 9.____
10. Everyone has left but they. 10.____

KEY (CORRECT ANSWERS)

1.	A	6.	A
2.	D	7.	B
3.	D	8.	A
4.	A	9.	D
5.	A	10.	D

TEST 8

DIRECTIONS: Each of the sentences in this test may be classified under one of the following four categories:
- A. Faulty because of incorrect grammar or word usage
- B. Faulty because of incorrect punctuation
- C. Faulty because of incorrect capitalization or incorrect spelling
- D. Correct

Examine each sentence carefully to determine under which of the above four options it is best classified. Then, in the space to the right, print the capital letter preceding the option which is the BEST of the four suggested above. (Note that each faulty sentence contains but one type of error. Consider a sentence to be correct if it contains none of the types of errors mentioned, even though there may be other correct ways of expressing the same thought.)

1. Who did we give the order to?   1.____
2. Send your order in immediately.   2.____
3. I believe I paid the Bill.   3.____
4. I have not met but one person.   4.____
5. Why aren't Tom, and Fred, going to the dance?   5.____
6. What reason is there for him not going?   6.____
7. The seige of Malta was a tremendous event.   7.____
8. I was there yesterday I assure you   8.____
9. Your ukulele is better than mine.   9.____
10. No one was there only Mary.   10.____

KEY (CORRECT ANSWERS)

1.	A	6.	A
2.	D	7.	C
3.	C	8.	B
4.	A	9.	C
5.	B	10.	A

TEST 9

DIRECTIONS: In each of the following groups of sentences, one of the four sentences is faulty in grammar, punctuation, or capitalization. Select the INCORRECT sentence in each case.

1. A. If you had stood at home and done your homework, you would not have failed in arithmetic.
   B. Her affected manner annoyed every member of the audience.
   C. How will the new law affect our income taxes?
   D. The plants were not affected by the long, cold winter, but they succumbed to the drought of summer.

   1.____

2. A. He is one of the most able men who have been in the Senate.
   B. It is he who is to blame for the lamentable mistake.
   C. Haven't you a helpful suggestion to make at this time?
   D. The money was robbed from the blind man's cup.

   2.____

3. A. The amount of children in this school is steadily increasing.
   B. After taking an apple from the table, she went out to play.
   C. He borrowed a dollar from me.
   D. I had hoped my brother would arrive before me.

   3.____

4. A. Whom do you think I hear from every week?
   B. Who do you think is the right man for the job?
   C. Who do you think I found in the room?
   D. He is the man whom we considered a good candidate for the presidency.

   4.____

5. A. Quietly the puppy laid down before the fireplace.
   B. You have made your bed; now lie in it.
   C. I was badly sunburned because I had lain too long in the sun.
   D. I laid the doll on the bed and left the room.

   5.____

KEY (CORRECT ANSWERS)

1. A
2. D
3. A
4. C
5. A

PREPARING WRITTEN MATERIAL
EXAMINATION SECTION
TEST 1

DIRECTIONS: Each short paragraph below is followed by four restatements or summaries of the information contained within it. Select the one that most completely and accurately states the information or opinion given in the paragraph. *PRINT THE LETTER OF THE CORRECT ANSWER IN THE SPACE AT THE RIGHT.*

1. Australia's koalas live solely on a diet of the leaves of the eucalyptus tree, a low-protein food that requires a koala to eat about three or four pounds of leaves a day. For most mammals, these strong-smelling leaves, saturated with toxins such as phenols and the oily compound known as cineole, are among the least digestible foods on the planet. However, the koala is equipped with a digestive system that is able to handle these toxins, trapping the tiniest leaf particles for as much as eight days while the sugars, proteins, and fats are extracted.   1.____
    A. Because eucalyptus leaves contain a large amount of toxins and oils, it takes a long time for koalas to digest them.
    B. Koalas have to eat three or four pounds of eucalyptus leaves a day, because the leaves are so poor in nutrients.
    C. Koalas have a unique digestive system that allows them to exist solely on a diet of eucalyptus leaves, which are generally toxic and inedible.
    D. The digestive system of the koala illustrates the unique evolutionary palette of the Australian continent.

2. Norway's special geopolitical position—it was the only NATO country to share a border with Russia—drove it to adopt much more cautious policies than other European countries during the Cold War. Its decision to join NATO led to strong protests from Russia, and in order to avoid provocation, Norway's foreign policy had to balance the need for ensuring defense capability with the need to keep tensions at the lowest possible level. Norway's low-tension "base policy" made clear the nation's refusal to allow foreign military forces on Norwegian territory as long as the country is not attacked or threatened with an attack.   2.____
    A. Norway's "base policy," in spite of its shared border with Russia, is the work of a pacifist nation that should serve as a model for foreign diplomacy everywhere.
    B. When Norway joined NATO, Russia feared a ground invasion over their shared border.
    C. The "base policy" of Norway is a perfect illustration on how much of Europe during the Cold War was a powder keg ready to explode at the slightest provocation.
    D. As the only member of the NATO alliance to border on Russia, Norway was forced to adopt a more conciliatory foreign policy than other members of the alliance.

3. During the women's suffrage movement of the early twentieth century, it was typical of many psychologists and anti-suffragists to automatically associate feminism with mental illness. In 1918, H.W. Frink wrote of feminists: "A certain proportion of at least the most militant suffragists are neurotics who in some instances are compensating for masculine trends, in others, are more or less successfully sublimating sadistic and homosexual ones." In the United States, anti-suffragists, finding comfort in psychology, concluded that suffragists all bordered hysteria and, thus, their arguments could not be taken seriously,
   A. The relationship between suffragism and feminism led many scientists to conclude that suffragists were afflicted with some kinds of mental illness.
   B. During the women's suffrage movement, anti-suffragists such as H.W. Frink tended to label women who fought for voting rights as mentally ill in order to dismiss their arguments.
   C. Responses to the women's suffrage movement are indicative of the tendency to label those who challenge the status quo as "Crazy" than to comfort their arguments.
   D. Most of the women who fought for suffrage during the early twentieth century were feminists who were mentally ill.

3._____

4. All of the earth's early plant life lived in the ocean, and most of these plants were concentrated in the shallow coastal waters, where the sun's energy could be easily absorbed. Because of the constant advance and retreat of tides in these regions, the plants—mostly algae—were repeatedly exposed to the atmosphere, and were forced to adapt to life out of water. It took millions of years before plant species had evolved that could survive out of the sea altogether, with stems that drew water from the ground, and a waxy covering to keep them from drying in the sun.
   A. After spending millions of years underwater, the earth's plants finally evolved ways of surviving on land.
   B. Most algaes today, because of evolutionary advances, are able to survive for extended periods of time out of water.
   C. Despite the fact that plants began as purely underwater organisms, they have always needed the sun's energy to survive.
   D. Land plants evolved from sea plants after millions of years in response to the gradual warming of the earth's atmosphere.

4._____

5. Because of the unique convergence of mild temperature and abundant rain (17 feet a year), British Columbia's temperate coastal rainforest is the most biologically productive ecosystem on earth. It's also an increasingly rare and vulnerable ecosystem: in its Holocene heyday, it covered only 0.2 percent of the earth's land surface. Today, logging and other development have consumed more than half this original range.
   A. The uniquely productive ecosystem of British Columbia's coastal rainforest has always been small, and has been reduced by human activity.
   B. Despite the fact that it is the most biologically productive ecosystem on earth, the coastal rainforest of British Columbia has been largely ignored by environmental activists.

5._____

C. The coastal rainforests of British Columbia have been nearly devastated by logging and other development.
D. British Columbia's coastal rainforest originated during the Holocene Era, but has declined steadily ever since.

6. The Roman Empire, which ruled much of the Western world for hundreds of years, was led by an aristocratic class famous for its tendency to drink large amounts of wine. Recently, an American medical researcher theorized that this taste for wine was eventually what caused the decline and fall of the empire—not the drinking of the wine itself, but a gradual poisoning from the lead that was used to line and seal Roman wine casks. The researcher, Dr. S.C. Gilfillan, argues that this lead poisoning specifically affected members of the Empire's ruling class, because they were the Romans most likely to consume wine and other products, like preserved fruits, that were stored in lead-lined jars.

6.____

A. The Roman aristocracy's taste for wine and dried fruits, according to one researcher, is a cautionary tale about the consequences of overindulgence.
B. While the Roman Empire's ruling class suffered from widespread lead poisoning, most commoners remained in good health throughout the empire.
C. One of the most far-fetched theories about the fall of the Roman Empire concerns itself with the lead used to line the wine casks and fruit jars of the ruling class.
D. An American medical researcher has theorized that the fall of the Roman Empire was caused by slow poisoning from the lead used to line and seal Roman wine casks and fruit jars.

7. In the second century B.C., King Hiero of Syracuse called upon the renowned scientist, Archimedes, to find a way to see if his crown was made of pure gold or a combination of metals. Archimedes came upon the solution some time later, as he was entering a tub full of hot water and noticed that the weight of his body displaced a certain amount of water. Realizing that this same principle could be used on the crown, he forgot himself with excitement, jumping out of the tub and running naked through the town, yelling "Eureka! Eureka!"

7.____

A. Archimedes, in making his famous discovery, unknowingly contributed the word "Eureka!" to the English vocabulary.
B. The relative purity of gold can be determined by the amount of water it displaces when submerged.
C. Archimedes, after discovering the solution to a scientific problem while stepping into his tub, became so excited that he ran through the town naked.
D. The word "Eureka" has become a part of the English language because of an interesting story involving the ancient scientist, Archimedes.

8. In the nineteenth century most Americans had never heard of, let alone tasted, an abalone, the marine mollusk considered to be a delicacy by many Asians, and undisturbed abalone populations thrived all along the west coast. When the California Gold Rush of the 1840s and 1850s brought thousands of Asian

8.____

immigrants to America, many of these people began to harvest the dense beds of abalone that inhabited the state's intertidal zone. The Asian harvests eventually brought in annual catches of over 4 million pounds of abalone, and as a result, some county governments passed ordinances making it illegal to dive for abalone in waters less than twenty feet deep.
   A. The Asians who immigrated to California during the Gold Rush harvested so much abalone from intertidal waters that some governments were compelled to limit abalone diving.
   B. Abalone diving was unheard of in California before the Gold Rush, when many Asians immigrated to the state and began to harvest abalone from the intertidal zone.
   C. The extreme shortage of abalone in California's intertidal waters can be traced to the Asians who immigrated during the Gold Rush.
   D. The abalone of California's coastal waters generally live in waters less than twenty feet deep, where they are not protected by most county governments.

9. Maria Tallchief, the daughter of a full-blood Osage Indian from Oklahoma, was America's first internationally celebrated prima ballerina, rising to stardom at a time when classical American ballet was still struggling to gain international acceptance and acclaim. Her innovative interpretations of such classics as "Swan Lake" and "The Nutcracker" helped convince critics worldwide that American ballet was a force to be reckoned with, and her glamorous beauty helped popularize ballet in America at a time when very few people took it seriously.
   A. As ballet grew more popular in America, Maria Tallchief became a phenomenon in Europe, helping to secure a worldwide reputation for excellence for American ballet.
   B. Nobody in America took ballet seriously until the beautiful Maria Tallchief became an international star.
   C. With her beauty and technical innovations, Maria Tallchief gained unprecedented critical and popular success for American ballet.
   D. Before the success of Maria Tallchief, there were not many ballet dancers in the United States worth noticing.

9._____

10. Early in the Constitutional Convention of 1787, the idea of a two-tiered legislature was agreed upon by the framers of the Constitution. The final form of each of the resulting houses, however, was an issue that was debated openly, and which was finally resolved by the "great compromise" of the Constitutional Convention. While the House of Representatives was intended to be a large, politically sensitive body, the Senate was designed to be a moderating influence that would check the powers of the House.
   A. The framers of the Constitution could not agree on whether the nation's legislature should be bicameral, or two-tiered, at first, but after the "great compromise," they devised a House and Senate.
   B. The Constitutional Convention of 1787 ended with the "great compromise" that gave the nation its two-tiered legislature.

10._____

C. After much behind-the-scenes dealmaking, the two-tiered legislature of the United States was devised by the framers of the Constitution.
D. The framers of the Constitution, after some debate, decided on a two-tiered legislature made up of a House of Representatives and a Senate that was less susceptible to regional politics.

11. Although scientists have succeeded in creating robots able to process huge amounts of information, they are still struggling to create one whose reasoning ability matches that of a human baby. The main challenge facing these scientists is the difficulty of understanding and imitating the complex process of human perception and reasoning, which involve the ability to register and analyze even the smallest changes in the external environment, and then to act on those changes.
    A. Even the most sophisticated robot is unable to imitate innate human abilities such as learning to walk, converse, or perceive depth.
    B. Because of their inability to process large amounts of information, robots have yet to achieve even the most fundamental level of reasoning.
    C. Despite considerable technological advances, scientists have as yet been unable to produce a robot that can respond intelligently to changes in its environment.
    D. Because robots cannot automatically filter out all extraneous information and focus on the most important details of a given situation, they are unable to reason as well as humans.

12. Thor Heyerdahl, a Norwegian anthropologist, had long held the opinion that the Polynesian inhabitants of South Pacific islands such as Samoa, Tonga, and Fiji had actually been migrants from South America. To prove that this was possible, in 1947 Heyerdahl made a crude raft out of balsa wood, which he named after an Incan sun god, *Kon-Tiki*, and sailed from the coast of Peru to the islands east of Tahiti
    A. Thor Heyerdahl's 1947 voyage on the *Kon-Tiki* proved that Polynesians probably had common ancestors in South America.
    B. While Thor Heyerdahl's *Kon-Tiki* voyage suggested a South American origin for Polynesians, most experts today believe the great migrations were launched from somewhere near Indonesia.
    C. To support the idea that Polynesians could have sailed from South America to the Pacific Islands, Thor Heyerdahl sailed the *Kon-Tiki* from Peru to Tahiti in 1947.
    D. Thor Heyerdahl's famous raft, the *Kon-Tiki*, was named for an Incan sun god, and was so well-made that it made it from Peru to Tahiti.

13. During the Age of Exploration, after thousands of miles of open sea, ships entered the bays of the Azore Islands, west of Portugal, with tattered sails, battered hulls, crewmen weakened from scurvy, and cargo holds laden with the treasure they had gained on their long trading journeys. Spanish, English, and Dutch warships prowled the waters around the Azores to protect this treasure, sometimes even sinking their own ships to keep it from falling into enemy

hands. During these fierce battles, many ships filled with treasure were sent to the ocean floor, where they still remain, preserved by the cold saltwater and centuries of rest.
- A. Although they are now sparsely populated, the Azore Islands were once a resting place for every ship returning from a long journey to the Americas.
- B. Many treasure hunters and archaeologists believe the sea floor around the Azores, a group of islands west of Portugal, still harbors some of the richest sunken treasure in the world.
- C. Economic competition between the European powers was so intense during the Age of Exploration that captains would rather sink their own ships rather than let their treasure fall into enemy hands.
- D. The rich history of the Azore Islands has deposited a large amount of sunken treasure in their surrounding waters.

14. The Whigs, a short-lived American political party, were wary of a domineering president, and many of them believed that the legislative branch should govern the nation. In particular, Whig leader Henry Clay often attempted to bully and belittle President John Tyler into submission. Tyler's resistance to Clay's high-handed tactics strengthened the office of the presidency, and in particular gave greater credibility to all later vice presidents who happened to succeed to the office.
    - A. While U.S. politics was at first dominated by the legislature, President John Tyler shifted the center of power to the presidency, while laying the groundwork for the downfall of the Whig Party.
    - B. President John Tyler, a failure by almost any other measure, can at least be credited with contributing to the strength of the presidency.
    - C. Henry Clay, who believed in a strong legislature, failed to win much influence over presidents who were not from the Whig Party.
    - D. President John Tyler, in resisting Henry Clay's bullying tactics, strengthened the U.S. presidency and lent credibility to the authority of vice presidential successors to the presidency.

14.____

15. By far the richest city on earth, Tokyo, Japan is also one of the most over-crowded; most of its people are only able to afford living in extremely small houses and apartments. In addition to cramped housing, Tokyo's overpopulation has created a commuter problem so grim that a corps of "pushers" has been hired by the city, to stand outside crowded commuter trains and help pack people inside. Problems such as these are so severe in Tokyo that there has been serious talk in recent years of moving Japan's capital elsewhere.
    - A. Despite the example of Tokyo, there is no evidence to suggest that economic wealth and overpopulation are related variables.
    - B. Tokyo's prosperity has led to such overcrowding that the country of Japan has recently begun to consider moving its capital to another location.
    - C. Despite being the richest city on earth, Tokyo, Japan is seriously overcrowded.
    - D. The small houses and apartments in Tokyo, along with its overcrowded transit system, are a perfect example of how economic wealth does not always improve a society's quality of life.

15.____

16. One of the greatest, and least publicized, legacies of Native American culture has been the worldwide cultivation of food staples through careful farming methods. Over centuries, tribes throughout North and South America domesticated the wild plants that have come to produce over half of the vegetables the world eats today. Corn, or maize, was first cultivated in the Mexican highlands almost seven thousand years ago, from a common wild grass called teosinte, and both potatoes and tomatoes were originally domesticated by the Peruvian Incas from native plants that still grow throughout Peru and Bolivia. 16.____
    A. Explorers of the Americas carried many native vegetables back to Europe, where they continued to adapt and flourish over the centuries.
    B. Today's common corn is a descendent of the wild Mexican teosinte plant, and potatoes and tomatoes were originally grown by the Incas.
    C. Without the agricultural knowledge and skill of early Native Americans, much of the world today would be in danger of famine.
    D. Foods that are today grown and eaten almost worldwide, such as corn, tomatoes, and potatoes, were first cultivated by the natives of North and South Americas.

17. America's transportation sector—95 percent of it driven by oil—consumes two-thirds of the petroleum used in the United States. With the 400 million cars now on the world's roads expected to grow to 1 billion by the year 2020, oil-foreign or not and other finite fossil-fuel resources will some day be conversation pieces for the nostalgic, rather than components of the nation's energy mix. 17.____
    A. In the future, most motor vehicles in the United States will be powered by an alternative energy source such as hydrogen or solar power.
    B. The continued growth of the oil-dependent transportation sector is outpacing the capacity of fossil-fuel energy resources.
    C. Our nation's dependence on foreign oil is a serious vulnerability that can only be corrected by increased domestic production.
    D. In the future, 1 billion cars across the world will be competing for oil and gasoline.

18. Althea Gibson, the first African-American to win the Wimbledon Tennis Championship, began her career by riding the subway out of her neighborhood in Harlem to 143rd Street, where she played paddle tennis against anyone who dared to challenge her. Since the Wimbledon tournament was played on grass, Gibson knew she would have to prepare herself by training on a surface that returned balls as quickly as a grass court. She found the solution to this problem in the gyms of Harlem, whose wood floors allowed her to perfect the rapid volley that helped her win two Wimbledon championships. 18.____
    A. Althea Gibson's tennis skills, including her famous volley, were developed in and around the inner-city neighborhood of Harlem.
    B. Althea Gibson had to leave her neighborhood to learn tennis, but to perfect her game, she had to return home to Harlem.
    C. Without the wood floors in the gyms of her Harlem neighborhood, Althea Gibson probably wouldn't have developed a volley that would help her win two Wimbledon tennis championships.

D. Although Althea Gibson achieved international fame as the first African-American to win the Wimbledon Tennis Championship, the path she followed to that championship was as unorthodox as the champion herself.

19. The greenhouse effect is a naturally occurring process that aids in heating the Earth's surface and atmosphere. It results from the fact that certain atmospheric gases, such as carbon dioxide, water vapor, and methane, are able to change the energy balance of the planet by being able to absorb longwave radiation from the Earth's surface. Without the greenhouse effect, life on this planet would probably not exist, as the average temperature of the Earth would be a chilly 5 degrees, rather than the present 59 degrees.
    A. The naturally-occurring greenhouse effect, by which atmospheric air is warmed, enables life to exist on earth.
    B. The greenhouse effect is a completely natural phenomenon that has nothing to do with human activity, and in fact it is beneficial to the planet's ecosystems.
    C. Human contributions to the increases in the greenhouse effect threaten life on Earth.
    D. In order for life to exist on Earth there must be some kind of greenhouse effect.

19.____

20. The religious and scientific communities have for centuries been at odds with each other, and held opposing viewpoints concerning the origin and nature of life. Progressive thinkers from both groups, however, claim that the two communities, in their ways of seeking answers to humanity's most important questions, share a common set of goals and procedures that would benefit greatly from a cooperative effort.
    A. Scientists and theologians will probably never agree on the origin and nature of life, though some progressive thinkers are trying to change the way the two communities talk about these issues.
    B. Though most scientists do not believe in God, progressive religious thinkers are continually trying to persuade them otherwise.
    C. Progressive religious and scientific thinkers have identified shared goals and questions that the two communities can work together to achieve and solve.
    D. Religious thinkers, who usually scorn such scientific theories as evolution, have begun to acknowledge the usefulness of science in answering important questions.

20.____

21. The administrations of Presidents Richard Nixon and Jimmy Carter oversaw an Export-Import Bank that was increasingly active in trade promotion, with expanding programs and lending authority. During this period, expenditures for program activities expanded to five times their 1969 rate, but the bank's net income dropped sharply—the low interest rates at which the bank financed its loan programs were lowering its profits.
    A. During the Nixon and Carter administrations, the budget of the Export-Import Bank grew to five times its 1969 expenditures.

21.____

B. Though the Export-Import Bank was very active during the Nixon and Carter administrations, its profits were reduced by its low interest rates.
C. Both the Nixon and Carter administrations demonstrated a lack of fiscal discipline that led to a declining net income at the Export-Import Bank.
D. Presidents Nixon and Carter both favored an activist Export-Import Bank, but while Nixon emphasized the function of trade promotion, Carter was more focused on making loans.

22. The Kombai and Korawai tribes of eastern Indonesia are known as the "tree people" for their custom of living in large tree houses, built as high as 150 feet above ground to avoid attacks from their enemies. These houses are built mostly from the fronds of the sago palm, a plant that also serves to produce one of the tree people's primary food sources—the larvae, or grub, of the scarab beetle. The tree people cultivate grubs by cutting a stretch of sago forest and then, after splitting and tying the palms together, leaving the palms to rot. 22.____
    A. The food-gathering methods of the Kombai and Korawai illustrate that deforestation is not a contemporary problem.
    B. The Kombai and Korawai people of eastern Indonesia relay on the sago palm for both food and housing.
    C. The Kombai and Korawai fears of enemy attacks have led them to build their trees high in the forest canopy
    D. Among the world's least-tamed native cultures are the Kombai and Korawai of Irian Jaya, the easternmost region of Indonesia.

23. It's no secret that corporate and federal information networks continue to deal with increasing bandwidth needs. The appetite for data—whether it's for internet access, file delivery, or the integration of digital voice applications—isn't likely to level off any time soon, and most information technology professionals allow that there is cause for concern. But emerging technologies for increasing raw bandwidth, accompanied by the streaming and maturing of transfer and switching protocols, are a good bet to accommodate the hunger for bandwidth, at least into the near future. 23.____
    A. There are two ways to decrease the demand for more bandwidth over computer networks: either increase the "raw" amount of bandwidth over an infrastructure, or devise more efficient transfer and switching protocols.
    B. Emerging technologies, aimed at the constantly increasing demand for bandwidth, are some day likely to result in virtually unlimited bandwidth for computer networks.
    C. Many different applications contribute to the demand for bandwidth over a computer network, and so the technologies that are devised to meet this demand must be many-faceted.
    D. While there is always a need for more bandwidth on large computer networks, newer technologies promise to increase the supply in the near term.

24. In the year 805, a Japanese Buddhist monk named Dengyo Daishi returned from his studies in China with some tea seeds, which he planted on a Japanese mountainside. In China, tea had long been the favorite drink of monks, because it helped them stay awake and attentive during their long periods of meditation, and Dengyo Daishi wanted to bring this practice to Japan. Over the centuries, tea-drinking would prove to be a custom that would influence nearly every aspect of Japanese culture, and Dengyo Daishi has long been considered a sort of saint among the Japanese.
    A. Because of the cultural similarities between China and Japan, it was only a matter of time before the ritual of tea-drinking made its way from the mainland to the island empire.
    B. Dengo Daishi, the first person to plant tea seeds in Japan, is revered among today's Japanese.
    C. The Japanese tea-drinking custom was begun in 805 by a Buddhist monk who brought tea seeds from China.
    D. Without the shared cultural traditions of Buddhism, it is unlikely that tea ever would have been imported from China to Japan.

24.____

25. Aztec women held a position in society that was far more respected than that of women in most Western civilizations of the time. For example, an Aztec wife was free to divorce a man who failed to provide for their children, or who was physically abusive, and once divorced, a woman was free to remarry whomever she chose. Perhaps the unusually high regard for Aztec women is best illustrated by the traditional Aztec religious belief that a special, elevated status in the afterlife was reserved for only two types of Aztec citizens-warriors who had died defending their tribe, and woman who had died during childbirth.
    A. The rights and privileges of Aztec women demonstrate that they were more respected by their societies than women of many cultures of the time.
    B. In the Aztec culture, women had the same rights and status as the most exalted men.
    C. Though the rights of Aztec women were still generally inferior to those of men, most Aztec women were granted a high degree of independence due to their service to the community.
    D. The relatively high position that Aztec women held in their society reveals the Aztec culture to be well ahead of its time.

25.____

KEY (CORRECT ANSWERS)

1.	C	11.	C
2.	D	12.	C
3.	B	13.	D
4.	A	14.	D
5.	A	15.	B
6.	D	16.	D
7.	C	17.	B
8.	A	18.	A
9.	C	19.	A
10.	D	20.	C

21.	B
22.	B
23.	D
24.	C
25.	A

PREPARING WRITTEN MATERIAL

PARAGRAPH REARRANGEMENT
COMMENTARY

The sentences that follow are in scrambled order. You are to rearrange them in proper order and indicate the letter choice containing the correct answer at the space at the right.

Each group of sentences in this section is actually a paragraph presented in scrambled order. Each sentence in the group has a place in that paragraph; no sentence is to be left out. You are to read each group of sentences and decide upon the best order in which to put the sentences so as to form a well-organized paragraph.

The questions in this section measure the ability to solve a problem when all the facts relevant to its solution are not given.

More specifically, certain positions of responsibility and authority require the employee to discover connection between events sometimes, apparently, unrelated. In order to do this, the employee will find it necessary to correctly infer that unspecified events have probably occurred or are likely to occur. This ability becomes especially important when action must be taken on incomplete information.

Accordingly, these questions require competitors to choose among several suggested alternatives, each of which presents a different sequential arrangement of the events. Competitors must choose the MOST logical of the suggested sequences.

In order to do so, they may be required to draw on general knowledge to infer missing concepts or events that are essential to sequencing the given events. Competitors should be careful to infer only what is essential to the sequence. The plausibility of the wrong alternatives will always require the inclusion of unlikely events or of additional chains of events which are NOT essential to sequencing the given events.

It's very important to remember that you are looking for the best of the four possible choices, and that the best choice of all may not even be one of the answers you're given to choose from.

There is no one right way to solve these problems. Many people have found it helpful to first write out the order of the sentences, as they would have arranged them, on their scrap paper before looking at the possible answers. If their optimum answer is there, this can save them some time. If it isn't, this method can still give insight into solving the problem. Others find it most helpful to just go through each of the possible choices, contrasting each as they go along. You should use whatever method feels comfortable and works for you.

While most of these types of questions are not that difficult, we've added a higher percentage of the difficult type, just to give you more practice. Usually there are only one or two questions on this section that contain such subtle distinctions that you're unable to answer confidently. And you then may find yourself stuck deciding between two possible choices, neither of which you're sure about.

EXAMINATION SECTION
TEST 1

DIRECTIONS: The sentences listed below are part of a meaningful paragraph, but they are not given in their proper order. You are to decide what would be the BEST order to put sentences to form a well-organized paragraph. Each sentence has a place in the paragraph; there are no extra sentences. *PRINT THE LETTER OF THE CORRECT ANSWER IN THE SPACE AT THE RIGHT.*

1.
   I. He came on a winter's eve.
   II. Akira came directly, breaking all tradition.
   III. He pounded on the door while a cold rain beat on the shuttered veranda, so at first Chie thought him only the wind.
   IV. Was that it?
   V. Had he followed form—had he asked his mother to speak to his father to approach a go-between—would Chie have been more receptive?
   The CORRECT answer is:
   A. II, IV, V, I, III   B. I, III, II, IV, V   C. V, IV, II, III, I   D. III, V, I, II, IV

   1._____

2.
   I. We have an understanding.
   II. Either method comes down to the same thing: a matter of parental approval.
   III. If you give your consent, I become Naomi's husband.
   IV. Please don't judge my candidacy by the unseemliness of this proposal.
   V. I ask directly because the use of a go-between takes much time.
   The CORRECT answer is:
   A. III, IV, II, V, I   B. I, V, II, III, IV   C. I, IV, V, II, III   D. V, III, I, IV, II

   2._____

3.
   I. Many relish the opportunity to buy presents because gift-giving offers a powerful means to build stronger bonds with one's closest peers.
   II. Aside from purchasing holiday gifts, most people regularly buy presents for other occasions throughout the year, including weddings, birthdays, anniversaries, graduations, and baby showers.
   III. Last year, Americans spent over $30 billion at retail stores in the month of December alone.
   IV. This frequent experience of gift-giving can engender ambivalent feelings in gift-givers.
   V. Every day, millions of shoppers hit the stores in full force—both online and on foot—searching frantically for the perfect gift.
   The CORRECT answer is:
   A. II, III, V, I, IV   B. IV, V, I, III, II   C. III, II, V, I, IV   D. V, III, II, IV, I

   3._____

4.
   I. Why do gift-givers assume that gift price is closely linked to gift-recipients' feelings of appreciation?
   II. Perhaps givers believe that bigger (i.e., more expensive) gifts convey stronger signals of thoughtfulness and consideration.
   III. In this sense, gift-givers may be motivated to spend more money on a gift in order to send a "stronger signal" to their intended recipient.
   IV. According to Camerer (1988) and others, gift-giving represents a symbolic ritual, whereby gift-givers attempt to signal their positive attitudes toward the intended recipient and their willingness to invest resources in a future relationship.
   V. As for gift-recipients, they may not construe smaller and larger gifts as representing smaller and larger signals of thoughtfulness and consideration.
   The CORRECT answer is:
   A. V, III, II, IV, I   B. I, II, IV, III, V   C. IV, I, III, V, II   D. II, V, I, IV, III

5.
   I. But when the spider is not hungry, the stimulation of its hairs merely causes it to shake the touched limb.
   II. Touching this body hair produces one of two distinct reactions.
   III. The entire body of a tarantula, especially its legs, is thickly clothed with hair.
   IV. Some of it is short and wooly, some long and stiff.
   V. When the spider is hungry, it responds with an immediate and swift attack.
   The CORRECT answer is:
   A. IV, II, I, III, V   B. V, I, III, IV, II   C. III, IV, II, V, I   D. I, II, IV, III, V

6.
   I. That tough question may be just one question away from an easy one.
   II. They tend to be arranged sequentially: questions on the first paragraph come before questions on the second paragraph.
   III. In summation, it is important not to forget that there is no penalty for guessing.
   IV. Try *all* questions on the passage.
   V. Remember, the critical reading questions after each passage are not arranged in order of difficulty.
   The CORRECT answer is:
   A. I, III, IV, II, V   B. II, I, V, III, IV   C. III, IV, I, V, II   D. V, II, IV, I, III

7.
   I. This time of year clients come to me with one goal in mind: losing weight.
   II. I usually tell them that their goal should be focused on fat loss instead of weight loss.
   III. Converting and burning fat while maintaining or building muscle is an art, which also happens to be my job.
   IV. What I love about this line of work is that *everyone* benefits from healthy eating and supplemental nutrition.
   V. This is because most of us have more stored fat than we prefer, but we do not want to lose muscle in addition to the fat.
   The CORRECT answer is:
   A. V, III, I, II, IV   B. I, IV, V, III, IV   C. II, I, III, IV, V   D. II, V, IV, I, II

8. I. In Tierra del Fuego, "invasive" describes the beaver perfectly.
    II. What started as a small influx of 50 beavers has since grown to a number over 200,000.
    III. Unlike in North America where the beaver has several natural predators that help to maintain manageable population numbers, Tierra del Fuego has no such luxury.
    IV. An invasive species is a non-indigenous animal, fungus, or plant species introduced to an area that has the potential to inflict harm upon the native ecosystem.
    V. It was first introduced in 1946 by the Argentine government in an effort to catalyze a fur trading industry in the region.
    The CORRECT answer is:
    A. IV, I, V, II, III   B. I, IV, II, III, V   C. II, V, III, I, IV   D. V, II, IV, III, I

8.____

9. I. The words ensure that we are all part of something much larger than the here and now.
    II. Literature might be thought of as the creative measure of history.
    III. It seems impossible to disconnect most literary works from their historical context.
    IV. Great writers, poets, and playwrights mold their sense of life and the events of their time into works of art.
    V. However, the themes that make their work universal and enduring perhaps do transcend time.
    The CORRECT answer is:
    A. I, III, II, V, IV   B. IV, I, V, II, III   C. II, IV, III, V, I   D. III, V, I, IV, II

9.____

10. I. If you don't already have an exercise routine, try to build up to a good 20- to 45-minute aerobic workout.
    II. When your brain is well oxygenated, it works more efficiently, so you do your work better and faster.
    III. Your routine will help you enormously when you sit down to work on homework or even on the day of a test.
    IV. Twenty minutes of cardiovascular exercise is a great warm-up before you start your homework.
    V. Exercise does not just help your muscles; it also helps your brain.
    The CORRECT answer is:
    A. I, IV, II, IV, III   B. IV, V, II, I, III   C. V, III, IV, II, I   D. III, IV, I, V, II

10.____

11. I. Experts often suggest that crime resembles an epidemic, but what kind?
    II. If it travels along major transportation routes, the cause is microbial.
    III. Economics professor Karl Smith has a good rule of thumb for categorizing epidemics: if it is along the lines of communication, he says the cause is information.
    IV. However, if it spreads everywhere all at once, the cause is a molecule.
    V. If it spreads out like a fan, the cause is an insect.
    The CORRECT answer is:
    A. I, III, II, V, IV   B. II, I, V, IV, III   C. V, III, I, II, IV   D. IV, V, I, III, II

11.____

12. I. A recent study had also suggested a link between childhood lead exposure and juvenile delinquency later on.
    II. These ideas all caused Nevin to look into other sources of lead-based items as well, such as gasoline.
    III. In 1994, Rick Nevin was a consultant working for the U.S Department of Housing and Urban Development on the costs and benefits of removing lead paint from old houses.
    IV. Maybe reducing lead exposure could have an effect on violent crime too?
    V. A growing body of research had linked lead exposure in small children with a whole raft of complications later in life, including lower IQ and behavioral problems.
    The CORRECT answer is:
    A. I, III, V, II, IV   B. IV, I, II, V, III   C. I, III, V, IV, II   D. III, V, I, IV, II

13. I. Like Lord Byron a century earlier, he had learn to play himself, his own best hero, with superb conviction.
    II. Or maybe he was Tarzan Hemingway, crouching in the African bush with elephant gun at the ready.
    III. He was Hemingway of the rugged outdoor grin and the hairy chest posing beside the lion he had just shot.
    IV. But even without the legend, the chest-beating, wisecracking pose that was later to seem so absurd, his impact upon us was tremendous.
    V. By the time we were old enough to read Hemingway, he had become legendary.
    The CORRECT answer is:
    A. I, V, II, IV, III   B. II, I, III, IV, V   C. IV, II, V, III, I   D. V, I, III, II, IV

14. I. Why do the electrons that inhabit atoms jump around so strangely, from one bizarrely shaped orbital to another?
    II. And most importantly, why do protons, the bits that give atoms their heft and personality, stick together at all?
    III. Why are some atoms, like sodium, so hyperactive while others, like helium, are so aloof?
    IV. As any good contractor will tell you, a sound structure requires stable materials.
    V. But atoms, the building blocks of everything we know and love—brownies and butterflies and beyond—do not appear to be models of stability.
    The CORRECT answer is:
    A. IV, V, III, I, II   B. V, III, I, II, IV   C. I, IV, II, V, III   D. III, I, IV, II, V

15. I. Current atomic theory suggests that the strong nuclear force is most likely conveyed by massless particles called "gluons".
    II. According to quantum chromodynamics (QCD), protons and neutrons are composed of smaller particles called quarks, which are held together by the gluons.
    III. As a quantum theory, it conceives of space and time as tiny chunks that occasionally misbehave, rather than smooth predictable quantities.

IV. If you are hoping that QCD ties up atomic behavior with a tidy little bow, you will be disappointed.
V. This quark-binding force has "residue" that extends beyond protons and neutrons themselves to provide enough force to bind the protons and neutrons together.

The CORRECT answer is:
A. III, IV, II, V, I   B. II, I, IV, III, V   C. I, II, V, IV, III   D. V, III, I, IV, II

16. I. I have seen him whip a woman, causing the blood to run half an hour at a time.
II. Mr. Severe, the overseer, used to stand by the door of the quarter, armed with a large hickory stick, ready to whip anyone who was not ready to start at the sound of the horn.
III. This was in the midst of her crying children, pleading for their mother's release.
IV. He seemed to take pleasure in manifesting his fiendish barbarity.
V. Mr. Severe was rightly named: he was a cruel man.

The CORRECT answer is:
A. I, IV, III, II, I   B. II, V, I, III, IV   C. II, V, III, I, IV   D. IV, III, I, V, II

16.____

17. I. His death was recorded by the slaves as the result of a merciful providence.
II. His career was cut short.
III. He died very soon after I went to Colonel Lloyd's; and he died as he lived, uttering bitter curses and horrid oaths.
IV. Mr. Severe's place was filled by a Mr. Hopkins.
V. From the rising till the going down of the sun, he was cursing, raving, cutting, and slashing among the slaves in the field.

The CORRECT answer is:
A. V, II, III, I, IV   B. IV, I, III, II, V   C. III, I, IV, V, II   D. I, II, V, III, IV

17.____

18. I. The primary reef-building organisms are invertebrate animals known as corals.
II. They are located in warm, shallow, tropical marine waters with enough light to stimulate the growth of reef organisms.
III. Coral reefs are highly diverse ecosystems, supporting greater numbers of fish species than any other marine ecosystem.
IV. They belong to the class Anthozoa and are subdivided into stony corals, which have six tentacles.
V. These corals are small colonial, marine invertebrates.

The CORRECT answer is:
A. I, IV, V, II, III   B. V, I, III, IV, II   C. III, II, I, V, IV   D. IV, V, II, III, I

18.____

19. I. Jane Goodall, an English ethologist, is famous for her studies of the chimpanzees of the Gombe Stream Reserve in Tanzania.
II. As a result of her studies, Goodall concluded that chimpanzees are an advanced species closely related to humans.
III. Ultimately, Goodall's observations led her to write *The Chimpanzee Family Book*, which conveys a new, more humane view of wildlife.

19.____

IV. She is credited with the first recorded observation of chimps eating meat and using and making tools.
V. Her observations have forced scientists to redefine the characteristics once considered as solely human traits.
The CORRECT answer is:
A. V, II, IV, III, I   B. I, IV, II, V, III   C. I, II, V, IV, III   D. III, V, II, I, IV

20. I. Since then, research has demonstrated that the deposition of atmospheric chemicals is causing widespread acidification of lakes, streams, and soil.
II. "Acid rain" is a popularly used phrase that refers to the deposition of acidifying substances from the atmosphere.
III. This phenomenon became a prominent issue around 1970.
IV. Of the many chemicals that are deposited from the atmosphere, the most important in terms of causing acidity in soil and surface waters are dilute solutions of sulfuric and nitric acids.
V. These chemicals are deposited as acidic rain or snow and include sulfur dioxide, oxides of nitrogen, and tiny particulates such as ammonium sulfate.
The CORRECT answer is:
A. III, IV, I, II, V   B. IV, III, I, IV, V   C. V, I, IV, III, II   D. II, III, I, IV, V

20.____

21. I. Programmers wrote algorithmic software that precisely specified both the problem and how to solve it.
II. AI programmers, in contrast, have sought to program computers with flexible rules for seeking solutions to problems.
III. In the 1940 and 1950s, the first large, electronic, digital computers were designed to perform numerical calculations set up by a human programmer.
IV. The computers did so by completing a series of clearly defined steps, or algorithms.
V. An AI program may be designed to modify the rules it is given or to develop entirely new rules.
The CORRECT answer is:
A. I, III, II, V, IV   B. IV, I, III, V, II   C. III, IV, I, II, V   D. III, I, II, IV, V

21.____

22. I. Wildfire is a periodic ecological disturbance, associated with the rapid combustion of much of the biomass of an ecosystem.
II. Wildfires themselves are both routine and ecologically necessary.
III. It is where they encounter human habitation, of course, that dangers quickly escalate,
IV. Once ignited by lightning or by humans, the biomass oxidizes as an uncontrolled blaze.
V. This unfettered burning continues until the fire either runs out of fuel or is quenched.
The CORRECT answer is:
A. V, IV, I, II, III   B. I, II, V, III, IV   C. III, II, I, IV, V   D. IV, V, III, I, II

22.____

23. I. His arguments supported the positions advanced by the Democratic Party's southern wing and sharply challenged the constitutionality of the Republican Party's emerging political platform.
    II. Beginning in the mid-1840s as a simple freedom suit, the case ended with the Court's intervention in the central political issues of the 1850s and the intensification of the sectional crisis that ultimately led to civil war.
    III. During the Civil War, the decision quickly fell into disrepute, and its major rulings were overruled by ratification of the 13th and 14th Amendments.
    IV. *Dred Scott v. Sandford* ranks as one of the worst decisions in the Supreme Court's history.
    V. Chief Justice Roger Taney, speaking for a deeply divided Court, brought about this turn of events by ruling that no black American—whether free or enslaved—could be a U.S. citizen and that Congress possessed no legitimate authority to prohibit slavery's expansion into the federal territories.
    The CORRECT answer is:
    A. II, IV, I, III, V   B. V, I, III, IV, II   C. I, V, II, V, III   D. IV, II, V, I, III

24. I. Considered the last battle between the U.S. Army and American Indians, the Wounded Knee Massacre took place on the morning of 29 December 1890 beside Wounded Knee Creek on South Dakota's Pine Ridge Reservation.
    II. This was the culmination of the Ghost Dance religion that had started with a Paiute prophet from Nevada named Wovoka (1856-1932), who was also known as Jack Wilson.
    III. During the previous year, U.S. government officials had reduced Sioux lands and cut back rations so severely that the Sioux people were starving.
    IV. These conditions encouraged the desperate embrace of the Ghost Dance.
    V. This pan-tribal ritual had historical antecedents that go much further back than its actual founder.
    The CORRECT answer is:
    A. I, II, III, IV, V   B. V, IV, II, III, I   C. IV, III, I, V, II   D. III, I, V, II, IV

25. I. Their actions, which became known as the Boston Tea Party, set in motion events that led directly to the American Revolution.
    II. Urged on by a crowd of cheering townspeople, the disguised Bostonians destroyed 342 chests of tea estimated to be worth between $10,000 an $18,000.
    III. The Americans, who numbered around 70, shared a common aim: to destroy the ships' cargo of British East India Company tea.
    IV. Many years later, George Hewes, a 31-year-old shoemaker and participant, recalled "We then were ordered by our commander to open the hatches and take out all the chests of tea and throw them overboard. And we immediately proceeded to execute his orders, first cutting and splitting the chests with our tomahawks, so as thoroughly to expose them to the effects of the water.

V. At nine o'clock on the night of December 16, 1773, a band of Bostonians disguised as Native Americans boarded the British merchant ship Dartmouth and two companion vessels anchored at Griffin's Wharf in Boston harbor.

The CORRECT answer is:

A. V, III, IV, II, I   B. IV, II, III, I, V   C. III, IV, V, II, I   D. V, II, IV, III, I

KEY (CORRECT ANSWERS)

1. A
2. C
3. D
4. B
5. C

6. D
7. B
8. A
9. C
10. B

11. A
12. D
13. D
14. A
15. C

16. B
17. A
18. C
19. B
20. D

21. C
22. B
23. D
24. A
25. A

TEST 2

DIRECTIONS: The sentences listed below are part of a meaningful paragraph, but they are not given in their proper order. You are to decide what would be the BEST order to put sentences to form a well-organized paragraph. Each sentence has a place in the paragraph; there are no extra sentences. *PRINT THE LETTER OF THE CORRECT ANSWER IN THE SPACE AT THE RIGHT.*

1.
   I. Recently, some U.S. cities have added a new category: compost, organic matter such as food scraps and yard debris.
   II. For example, paper may go in one container, glass and aluminum in another, regular garbage in a third.
   III. Like paper or glass recycling, composting demands a certain amount of effort from the public in order to be successful.
   IV. Over the past generation, people in many parts of the United States have become accustomed to dividing their household waste products into different categories for recycling.
   V. But the inconveniences of composting are far outweighed by its benefits.
   The CORRECT answer is:
   A. V, II, III, IV, I   B. I, III, IV, V, II   C. IV, II, I, III, V   D. III, I, V, II, IV

   1.____

2.
   I. It also enhances soil texture, encouraging healthy roots and minimizing the need for chemical fertilizers.
   II. Most people think of banana peels, eggshells, and dead leaves as "waste," but compost is actually a valuable resource with multiple practical uses.
   III. When utilized as a garden fertilizer, compost provides nutrients to soil and improves plant growth while deterring or killing pests and preventing some plant diseases.
   IV. In large quantities, compost can be converted into a natural gas that can be used as fuel for transportation or heating and cooling systems.
   V. Better than soil at holding moisture, compost minimizes water waste and storm runoff, increases savings on watering costs, and helps reduce erosion on embankments near bodies of water.
   The CORRECT answer is:
   A. II, III, I, V, IV   B. I, IV, V, III, II   C. V, II, IV, I, III   D. III, V, II, IV, I

   2.____

3.
   I. The street is a sea of red, the traditional Chinese color of luck and happiness.
   II. Buildings are draped with festive, red banners and garlands.
   III. Crowds gather then to celebrate Lunar New Year.
   IV. Lamp posts are strung with crimson paper lanterns, which bob in the crisp winter breeze.
   V. At the beginning of February, thousands of people line H Street, the heart of Chinatown in Washington, D.C.
   The CORRECT answer is:
   A. I, V, II, III, IV   B. IV, II, V, I, III   C. III, I, II, IV, V   D. V, III, I, II, IV

   3.____

4. I. Experts agree that the lion dance originated in the Han dynasty; however, there is little agreement about the dance's original purpose.
    II. Another theory is that an emperor, upon waking from a dream about a lion, hired an artist to choreograph the dance.
    III. Dancers must be synchronized with the music accompanying the dance, as well as with each other, in order to fully realize the celebration.
    IV. Whatever the origins are, the current function of the dance is celebration.
    V. Some evidence suggests that the earliest version of the dance was an attempt to ward off an evil spirt.
    The CORRECT answer is:
    A. V, II, IV, III, I   B. I, V, II, IV, III   C. II, I, III, V, IV   D. IV, III, V, I, II

    4.____

5. I. Half the population of New York, Toronto, and London do not own cars; instead they use public transport.
    II. Every day, subway systems carry 155 million passengers, thirty-four times the number carried by all the world's airplanes.
    III. Though there are 600 million cars on the planet, and counting, there are also seven billion people, which means most of us get around taking other modes of transportation.
    IV. All of that is to say that even a century and a half after the invention of the internal combustion engine, private car ownership is still an anomaly.
    V. In other words, traveling to work, school, or the market means being a straphanger: someone who relies on public transport.
    The CORRECT answer is:
    A. I, II, IV, V, III   B. III, V, I, II, IV   C. III, I, II, IV, V   D. II, IV, V, III, I

    5.____

6. I. "They jumped up like popcorn," he said, describing how they would flap their half-formed wings and take short hops into the air.
    II. Dan settled on the Chukar Partridge as a model species, but he might not have made his discovery without the help of a local rancher that supplied him with the birds.
    III. At field sites around the world, Dan Kiel saw a pattern in how young ground birds ran along behind their parents.
    IV. So when a group of graduate students challenged him to come up with new data on the age-old ground-up-tree-down debate, he designed a project to see what clues might lie in how baby game birds learned to fly.
    V. When the rancher stopped by to see how things were progressing, he yelled at Dan to give the birds something to climb on.
    The CORRECT answer is:
    A. IV, II, V, I, III   B. III, II, I, V, IV   C. III, I, IV, II, V   D. I, II, IV, V, III

    6.____

7. I. Honey bees are hosts to the pathogenic large ectoparasitic mite, *Varroa destructor*.
    II. These mites feed on bee hemolymph (blood) and can kill bees directly or by increasing their susceptibility to secondary infections.
    III. Little is known about the natural defenses that keep the mite infections under control.

    7.____

IV. Pyrethrums are a group of flowering plants that produce potent insecticides with anti-mite activity.
V. In fact, the human mite infestation known as scabies is treated with a topical pyrethrum cream.
The CORRECT answer is:
A. I, II, III, IV, V   B. V, IV, II, I, III   C. III, IV, V, I, II   D. II, IV, I, III, V

8.
I. He hardly ever allowed me to pay for the books he placed in my hands, but when he wasn't looking I'd leave the coins I'd managed to collect on the counter.
II. My favorite place in the whole city was the Sempere & Sons bookshop on Calle Santa Ana.
III. It smelled of old paper and dust and it was my sanctuary, my refuge.
IV. The bookseller would let me sit on a chair in a corner and read any book I liked to my heart's content.
V. It was only small change—if I'd had to buy a book with that pittance, I would probably have been able to afford only a booklet of cigarette papers.
The CORRECT answer is:
A. I, III, V, II, IV   B. II, IV, I, III, V   C. V, I, III, IV, II   D. II, III, IV, I, V

8.____

9.
I. At school, I had learned to read and write long before the other children.
II. My father, however, did not see things the way I did; he did not like to see books in the house.
III. Where my school friends saw notches of ink on incomprehensible pages, I saw light, streets, and people.
IV. Back then my only friends were made of paper and ink.
V. Words and the mystery of their hidden science fascinated me, and I saw in them a key with which I could unlock a boundless world.
The CORRECT answer is:
A. IV, I, III, V, II   B. I, V, III, IV, II   C. II, I, V, III, IV   D. V, IV, II, III, I

9.____

10.
I. Gary King of Harvard University says that one main reason null results are not published is because there were many ways to produce them by messing up.
II. Oddly enough, there is little hard data on how often or why null results are squelched.
III. The various errors make the null reports almost impossible to predict, Mr. King believes.
IV. In recent years, the debate has spread to social and behavioral science, which help sway public and social policy.
V. The question of what to do with null results in research has long been hotly debated among those conducting medical trials.
The CORRECT answer is:
A. I, III, IV, V, II   B. V, I, II, IV, III   C. III, II, I, V, IV   D. V, IV, II, I, III

10.____

11. I. In a recent study, Stanford political economist Neil Malholtra and two of his graduate students examined all studies funded by TESS (Time-sharing Experiments for Social Sciences).
    II. Scientists of these experiments cited deeper problems within their studies but also believed many journalists wouldn't be interested in their findings.
    III. TESS allows scientists to order up internet-based surveys of a representative sample of U.S. adults to test a particular hypothesis.
    IV. One scientist went on record as saying, "The reality is that null effects do not tell a clear story."
    V. Well, Malholtra's team tracked down working papers from most of the experiments that weren't published to find out what had happened to their results.
    The CORRECT answer is:
    A. IV, II, V, III, I   B. I, III, V, II, IV   C. III, V, I, IV, II   D. I, III, IV, II, V

    11._____

12. I. The work also suggests that these ultra-tiny salt wires may already exist in sea spray and large underground salt deposits.
    II. Scientists expect for metals such as gold or lead to stretch out at temperatures well below their melting points, but they never expected this superplasticity in a rigid, crystalline material like salt.
    III. Inflexible old salt becomes a softy in the nanoworld, stretching like taffy to more than twice its length, researchers report.
    IV. The findings may lead to new approaches for making nanowires that could end up in solar cells or electronic circuits.
    V. According to Nathan Moore of Sandia National Laboratories, these nanowires are special and much more common than we may think.
    The CORRECT answer is:
    A. IV, III, V, II, I   B. I, V, III, IV, II   C. III, IV, I, V, II   D. V, II, III, I, IV

    12._____

13. I. The Venus flytrap (Dionaea muscipula) needs to know when an ideal meal is crawling across its leaves.
    II. The large black hairs on their lobes allow the Venus flytraps to literally feel their prey, and they act as triggers that spring the trap closed.
    III. To be clear, if an insect touches just one hair, the trap will not spring shut; but a large enough bug will likely touch two hairs within twenty seconds which is the signal the Venus flytrap waits for.
    IV. Closing its trap requires a huge expense of energy, and reopening can take several hours.
    V. When the proper prey makes its way across the trap, the Dionaea launches into action.
    The CORRECT answer is:
    A. IV, I, V, II, III   B. II, V, I, III, IV   C. I, II, V, IV, III   D. I, IV, II, V, III

    13._____

14. I. These books usually contain collections of stories, many of which are much older than the books themselves.
    II. Where other early European authors wrote their literary works in Latin, the Irish began writing down their stories in their own language as early as 6th century B.C.E.
    III. Ireland has the oldest vernacular literature in Europe.
    IV. One of the most famous of these collections is the epic cycle, *The Táin Bó Cúailnge*, which translates to "The Cattle Raid of Cooley."
    V. While much of the earliest Irish writing has been lost or destroyed, several manuscripts survive from the late medieval period.
    The CORRECT answer is:
    A. V, IV, I, II, III   B. III, II, V, I, IV   C. III, I, IV, V, II   D. IV, II, III, I, V

14.____

15. I. Obviously the plot is thin, but it works better as a thematic peace, exploring several great issues that plagued authors and people during that era.
    II. The story begins during a raid when Meb's forces are joined by Frederick and his men.
    III. In the end, many warriors on both sides perish, the prize is lost, and peace is somehow re-established between the opposing sides.
    IV. The middle of the story tells of how Chulu fends off Meb's army by herself while Concho's men struggle against witchcraft.
    V. The prize is defended by the current king, Concho, and the young warrior, Chulu.
    The CORRECT answer is:
    A. II, V, IV, III, I   B. V, I, IV, III, II   C. I, III, V, IV, II   D. III, II, I, V, IV

15.____

16. I. However, sometimes the flowers that are treated with the pesticides are not as vibrant as those that did not receive the treatment.
    II. The first phase featured no pesticides and the second featured a pesticide that varied in doses.
    III. In the cultivation of roses, certain pesticides are often applied when the presence of aphids is detected.
    IV. Recently, researchers conducted two phases of an experiment to study the effects of certain pesticides on rose bushes.
    V. To start, aphids are small plant-eating insects known to feed on rose bushes.
    The CORRECT answer is:
    A. IV, III, II, I, V   B. I, II, V, III, IV   C. V, III, I, IV, II   D. II, V, IV, I, III

16.____

17. I. My passion for it took hold many years ago when I happened to cross paths with a hiker in a national park.
    II. The wilderness has a way of cleansing the spirit.
    III. His excitement was infectious as he quoted various poetic verses pertaining to the wild; I was hooked.
    IV. For some, backpacking is the ultimate vacation.
    V. While it once felt tedious and tiring, backpacking is now an essential part of my summer recreation.
    The CORRECT answer is:
    A. IV, II, V, I, III   B. II, III, I, IV, V   C. I, IV, II, V, III   D. V, I, III, II, IV

17.____

18.
   I. When I was preparing for my two-week vacation to southern Africa, I realized that the continent would be like nothing I have ever seen.
   II. I wanted to explore the continent's urban streets as well as the savannah; it's always been my dream to have "off the grid" experiences as well as touristy ones.
   III. The largest gap in understanding came from an unlikely source; it was the way I played with my host family's dog.
   IV. Upon my arrival to Africa, the people I met welcomed me with open arms.
   V. Aside from the pleasant welcome, it was obvious that our cultural differences were stark, which led to plenty of laughter and confusion.
   The CORRECT answer is:
   A. IV, I, II, III, V   B. III, V, IV, II, I   C. I, IV, II, III, V   D. I, II, IV, V, III

18.____

19.
   I. There, I signed up for a full-contact, downhill ice-skating race that looked like a bobsled run.
   II. It wasn't until I took a trip to Montreal that I realized how wrong I was.
   III. As an avid skier and inline skater, I figured I had cornered the market on downhill speeds.
   IV. After avoiding hip and body checks, both of which were perfectly legal, I was able to reach a top speed of forty-five miles per hour!
   V. It was Carnaval season, the time when people from across the province flock to the city for two weeks of food, drink and winter sports.
   The CORRECT answer is:
   A. II, I, III, IV, V   B. III, II, V, I, IV   C. IV, V, I, III, II   D. I, IV, II, V, III

19.____

20.
   I. It is a spell that sets upon one's soul and a sense of euphoria is felt by all who experience it.
   II. Pictures and postcards of the Caribbean do not lie; the water there shines with every shade of aquamarine, from pastel to emerald.
   III. As I imagine these sights, I recall one trip in particular that neatly captures the allure of the Caribbean.
   IV. The ocean hypnotizes with its glassy vastness.
   V. On that beautiful day, I was incredibly happy to sail with my family and friends.
   The CORRECT answer is:
   A. I, V, IV, III, II   B. V, I, II, IV, III   C. II, IV, I, III, V   D. I, II, IV, III, V

20.____

21.
   I. It wasn't until the early 1700s that it began to resemble the masterpiece museum it is today.
   II. The Louvre contains some of the most famous works of art in the history of the world including the *Mona Lisa* and the *Venus de Milo*.
   III. Before it was a world famous museum, The Louvre was a fort built by King Philip sometime around 1200 A.D.
   IV. The Louvre, in Paris, France, is one of the largest museums in the world.
   V. It has almost 275,000 works of art, which are displayed in over 140 exhibition rooms.
   The CORRECT answer is:
   A. V, I, III, IV, II   B. II, IV, I, V, III   C. V, III, I, IV, II   D. IV, V, II, III, I

21.____

22. I. It danced on the glossy hair and bright eyes of two girls, who sat together hemming ruffles for a white muslin dress.
    II. The September sun was glinting cheerfully into a pretty bedroom furnished with blue.
    III. These girls were Clover and Elsie Carr, and it was Clover's first evening dress for which they were hemming ruffles.
    IV. The half-finished skirt of the dress lay on the bed, and as each crisp ruffle was completed, the girls added it to the snowy heap, which looked like a drift of transparent clouds.
    V. It was nearly two years since a certain visit made by Johnnie to Inches Mills and more than three since Clover and Katy had returned home from the boarding school at Hillsover.
    The CORRECT answer is:
    A. III, V, IV, I, II   B. II, I, IV, III, V   C. V, II, I, IV, III   D. II, IV, III, I, V

23. I. The "invisible hand" theory is harshly criticized by parties who argue that untampered self-interest is immoral and that charity is the superior vehicle for community improvement.
    II. Standing as a testament to his benevolence, Smith bequeathed much of his wealth to charity.
    III. Second, Smith was not arguing that all self-interest is positive for society; he simply did not agree that it was necessarily bad.
    IV. First, he was not declaring that people should adopt a pattern of overt self-interest, but rather that people already act in such a way.
    V. Some of these people, though, fail to recognize several important aspects of Adam Smith's the Scottish economist who championed this theory, concept.
    The CORRECT answer is:
    A. I, V, IV, III, II   B. III, IV, II, I, V   C. II, III, V, IV, I   D. IV, III, I, V, II

24. I. Though they rarely are awarded for their many accomplishments, composers and performers continue to innovate and represent a substantial reason for classical music's persistent popularity.
    II. It is often the subject of experimentation on the part of composers and performers.
    III. Even more restrictive is the mainstream definition of "classical," which only includes the music of generations past that has seemingly been pushed aside by such contemporary forms of music as jazz, rock, and rap.
    IV. In spite of its waning limelight, however, classical music occupies an enduring niche in Western culture.
    V. Many people take classical music to be the realm of the symphony orchestra or smaller ensembles of orchestral instruments.
    The CORRECT answer is:
    A. IV, I, III, II, V   B. II, IV, V, I, III   C. V, III, IV, II, I   D. I, V, III, IV, II

25.
I. The Great Pyramid at Giza is arguably one of the most fascinating and contentious pieces of architecture in the world.
II. Instead of clarifying or expunging older theories about its age, the results of the study left the researchers mystified.
III. In the 1980s, researchers began focusing on studying the mortar from the pyramid, hoping it would reveal important clues about the pyramid's age and construction.
IV. This discovery was controversial because these dates claimed that the structure was built over 400 years earlier than most archaeologists originally believed it had been constructed.
V. Carbon dating revealed that the pyramid had been built between 3100 BCE and 2850 BCE with an average date of 2977 BCE.

The CORRECT answer is:
A. I, III, II, V, IV B. II, III, IV, V, I C. V, I, III, IV, II D. III, IV, V, I, II

25.____

KEY (CORRECT ANSWERS)

1.	C	11.	B
2.	A	12.	C
3.	D	13.	D
4.	B	14.	B
5.	B	15.	A
6.	C	16.	C
7.	A	17.	A
8.	D	18.	D
9.	A	19.	B
10.	D	20.	C

21. D
22. B
23. A
24. C
25. A

EXAMINATION SECTION
TEST 1

DIRECTIONS: The sentences listed below are part of a meaningful paragraph, but they are not given in their proper order. You are to decide what would be the BEST order to put sentences to form a well-organized paragraph. Each sentence has a place in the paragraph; there are no extra sentences. *PRINT THE LETTER OF THE CORRECT ANSWER IN THE SPACE AT THE RIGHT.*

Questions 1-3.

DIRECTIONS: Questions 1 through 3 are to be answered on the basis of the following passage.

Almost half of the increase in Chicago came from five neighborhoods, including West Garfield Park. He was 12 years old and had just been recruited into a gang by his older brothers and cousin. A decade later, he sits in Cook County jail, held without bail and awaiting trial on three cases, including felony drug charges and possession of a weapon. Violence in Chicago erupted last year, with the city recording 771 murders—a 58% jump from 2015. They point to a $95 million police-training center in West Garfield Park, public-transit improvements on Chicago's south side and efforts to get major corporations such as Whole Foods and Wal-Mart to invest. Chicago city officials say that they are making strategic investments in ailing neighborhoods. Amarley Coggins remembers the first time he dealt heroin, discreetly approaching a car coming off an interstate highway and into West Garfield park, the neighborhood where he grew up on Chicago's west side.

1. When organized correctly, the first sentence of the paragraph begins with 1.____
    A. "Amarley Coggins remembers..." B. "He was 12 years old..."
    C. "They point to a..." D. "Violence in Chicago..."

2. After correctly organizing the paragraph, the author wishes to replace a word 2.____
    in the last sentence with its synonym *enterprises*. Which word does the author wish to replace?
    A. murders B. neighborhoods
    C. corporations D. improvements

3. If put together correctly, the second to last sentence would end with the words 3.____
    A. "...Chicago's west side." B. "...in ailing neighborhoods."
    C. "...older brother and cousins." D. "...and Wal-Mart to invest."

Questions 4-6.

DIRECTIONS: Questions 4 through 6 are to be answered on the basis of the following passage.

Critics argue that driverless vehicles pose too many risks, including cyberattacks, computer malfunctions, relying on algorithms to make ethical decisions, and fewer transportation jobs. Driverless vehicles, also called autonomous vehicles and self-driving vehicles, are vehicles that can operate without human intervention. And algorithms make decisions based on data obtained from sensors and connectivity. Driverless vehicles rely primarily on three technologies: sensors, connectivity, and algorithms. Sensors observe multiple directions simultaneously. Connectivity accesses information on traffic, weather, road hazards, and navigation. Supporters argue that driverless vehicles have many benefits, including fewer traffic accidents and fatalities, more efficient traffic flows, greater mobility for those who cannot drive, and less pollution. Once the realm of science fiction, driverless vehicles could revolutionize automotive travel over the next few decades.

4. When all of the sentences are organized in correct order, the first sentence starts with
   A. "Connectivity accesses information..."
   B. "Critics argue that..."
   C. "Once the realm of..."
   D. "Driverless vehicles, also called..."

5. If the above paragraph appeared in correct order, which of the following transition words would be MOST appropriate in the beginning of the sentence that starts "Critics argue that..."
   A. Additionally
   B. To begin,
   C. In conclusion,
   D. Conversely,

6. When the paragraph is properly arranged, it ends with the words
   A. "...over the next few decades."
   B. "...fewer transportation jobs."
   C. "...and less pollution."
   D. "...without human intervention"

Questions 7-10.

DIRECTIONS: Questions 7 through 10 are to be answered on the basis of the following passage.

This method had some success, but also carried fatal risks. Various people across Europe independently developed vaccination as an alternative during the later years of the eighteenth century, but Edward Jenner (1749-1823) popularized the practice. Vaccination has been called a miracle of modern medicine, but it has a long and controversial history stretching back to the ancient world. In 1803 the Royal Jennerian Institute was founded in England, and vaccination programs initially drew enormous public support. In 429 BCE in Greece, the historian Thucydides (c.460-c.395 BCE) noted that survivors of smallpox did not become reinfected in subsequent epidemics. Variolation as a means of preventing severe smallpox infection became an accepted practice in China in the tenth century CE, and its popularity spread across Asia,

Europe, and to the Americas by the seventeenth century. Variolation required either inhalation of smallpox dust, or putting scabs or parts of the smallpox pustules under the skin. Widespread inoculation against smallpox was purported to have been part of Ayurvedic tradition as far back as at least 1000 BCE, when Indian doctors traveled to households before the rainy season each year.

7. When arranged properly, what does "This method" refer to in the sentence that begins "This method had some success..."?
   A. Vaccination
   B. Inoculation
   C. Variolation
   D. Hybridization

   7.____

8. When organized correctly, the paragraph's third sentence should begin
   A. "In 429 BCE in Greece..."
   B. "Variolation required..."
   C. "In 1803 the..."
   D. "Vaccination has been called..."

   8.____

9. If put in the correct order, this paragraph should end with the words
   A. "...under the skin."
   B. "...to the ancient world."
   C. "...enormous public support."
   D. "...by the seventeenth century."

   9.____

10. In the second sentence, the author is thinking about using the word immunization instead of which of its synonyms?
    A. Variolation   B. Vaccination   C. Inhalation   D. Inoculation

    10.____

Questions 11-13.

DIRECTIONS: Questions 11 through 13 are to be answered on the basis of the following passage.

Summers are hot—often north of 100 degrees—and because it lies at the far end of a San Diego Gas & Electric transmission line, the town has suffered frequent power outages. Another way is that microgrids can ease the entry of intermittent renewable energy sources, like wind and solar, into the modern grid. Utilities are also interested in microgrids because of the money they can save by deferring the need to build new transmission lines. "If you're on the very end of a utility line, everything that happens, happens 10 times worse for you," says Mike Gravely, team leader for energy systems integration at the California Energy Commission. The town has a lot of senior citizens, who can be frail in the heat. Borrego Springs, California, is a quaint town of about 3,400 people set against the Anza-Borrego Desert about 90 miles east of San Diego. High winds, lightning strikes, forest fires and flash floods can bust up that line and kill the electricity. But today, Borrego Springs has a failsafe against power outages: a microgrid. Resiliency is one of the main reasons the market in microgrids is booming, with installed capacity in the United States projected to be more than double between 2017 and 2022, according to a new report on microgrids from GTM Research. "Without air conditioning," says Linda Haddock, head of the local Chamber of Commerce, "people will die."

11. When the sentences above are organized correctly, the paragraph should start with the sentence that begins
    A. "Borrego Springs, California..."
    B. "But today, Borrego Springs..."
    C. "Summers are hot..."
    D. "Utilities are also interested..."

    11.____

12. If the author wanted to split this paragraph into two smaller paragraphs, the first sentence of the second paragraph would start with the words
    A. "High winds, lightning strikes, forest fires…"
    B. "But today, Borrego Springs…"
    C. "Resiliency is one of the main…"
    D. "If you're on the very end…"

    12.____

13. Assuming the paragraph were organized correctly, the second to last sentence would end
    A. "…to build new transmission lines."
    B. "…be frail in the heat."
    C. "…into the modern grid."
    D. "…east of San Diego."

    13.____

Questions 14-17.

DIRECTIONS: Questions 14 through 17 are to be answered on the basis of the following passage.

Exhaustive search is not typically a successful approach to problem solving because most interesting problems have search spaces that are simply too large to be dealt with in this manner, even by the fastest computers. Thus, in order to ignore a portion of a search space, some guiding knowledge or insight must exist so that the solution will not be overlooked. This partial understanding is reflected in the fact that a rigid algorithmic solution—a routine and predetermined number of computational steps—cannot be applied. A large part of the intelligence of chess players resides in the heuristics they employ. When search is used to explore the entire solution space, it is said to be exhaustive. Chess is a classic example where humans routinely employ sophisticated heuristics in a search space. Therefore, if one hopes to find a solution (or a reasonably good approximation of a solution) to such a problem, one must selectively explore the problem's search space. Rather, the concept of search is used to solve such problems. Heuristics is a major area of AI that concerns itself with how to limit effectively the exploration of a search space. Many problems that humans are confronted with are not fully understood. The difficulty here is that if part of the search space is not explored, one runs the risk that the solution one seeks will be missed. A chess player will typically search through a small number of possible moves before selecting a move to play. Not every possible move and countermove sequence is explored. Only reasonable sequences are examined.

14. When correctly organized, the paragraph above should begin with the words
    A. "Many problems that…"
    B. "Therefore, if one hopes to…"
    C. "Only reasonable sequences are…"
    D. "The difficulty here is…"

    14.____

15. If the paragraph was organized correctly, the fourth sentence would begin with the words
    A. "Chess is a classic…"   B. "Heuristics is a major…"
    C. "Exhaustive search is not…"   D. "The difficulty here is…"

    15.____

16. If the author wished to separate this paragraph into two equally sized paragraphs, the sentence that begins the second paragraph would END with the words
    A. "...heuristics they employ."
    B. "...in a search space."
    C. "...are not fully employed."
    D. "...will be missed."

16.____

17. When organized correctly, the paragraph would end with the words
    A. "...the heuristics they employ."
    B. "...will not be overlooked."
    C. "...said to be exhaustive."
    D. "...are not fully understood."

17.____

Questions 18-21.

DIRECTIONS: Questions 18 through 21 are to be answered on the basis of the following passage.

Asian-Americans soon found themselves the targets of ridicule and attacks. Prior to the bombing he had tried to enlist in the military but was turned down due to poor health. His case, Korematsu v. The United States, is still considered a blemish on the record of the Supreme Court and has received heightened scrutiny given the indefinite confinement of many prisoners after the terrorist attacks on September 11, 2001. On February 19, 1942, President Franklin D. Roosevelt issued Executive Order 9066, which granted the leaders of the armed forces permission to create Military Areas and authorizing the removal of any and all persons from those areas. Fred Korematsu was a 22-year-old welder when the Japanese bombed Pearl Harbor on December 7, 1941. A Nisei—which means an American citizen born to Japanese parents—he was one of four brothers and grew up working in his parents' plant nursery in Oakland, California. This statement effectively pronounced Japanese-Americans on the West Coast as traitors because even though Executive Order 9066 allowed the military to remove any person from designated areas, only those of Japanese descent were ordered to leave. Before Pearl Harbor, he was employed by a defense contractor in California. At the time of the attack, he was having a picnic with his Italian-American girlfriend. Asian-American Fred Korematsu (1919-2005) is most remembered for challenging the legality of Japanese internment during World War II. It was for this simple reason that he eventually became known as a civil rights leader. American reaction to an attack on United States' soil was both swift and harsh. Awarded the Presidential Medal of Honor, he is considered a leader of the civil rights movement in the United States. Roosevelt justified these actions in the opening paragraph of the order by declaring, "the successful prosecution of the war requires every possible protection against espionage, and against sabotage to national-defense material, national-defenses premises and national-defense utilities." Years later he told the San Francisco Chronicle, "I was just living my life, and that's what I wanted to do."

18. When put together correctly, the above paragraph would begin with the words
    A. "It was for this simple reason..."
    B. "A Nisei—which means..."
    C. "Awarded the Presidential Medal of Honor..."
    D. "Asian-American Fred Korematsu..."

18.____

19. If the author wished to separate this piece into two separate paragraphs, the sentence that would be the BEST way to start the second paragraph would begin with the words
    A. "Awarded the Presidential Medal of Honor..."
    B. "Fred Korematsu was a..."
    C. "Roosevelt justified these actions..."
    D. "Before Pearl Harbor, he was..."

    19.____

20. In the sentence that begins "A Nisei—which means...", who does "he" refer to in the paragraph?
    A. Roosevelt
    B. A sibling of Korematsu
    C. Fred Korematsu
    D. Japanese-Americans on the West Coast

    20.____

21. If organized correctly, the fourth sentence should begin with the words
    A. "At the time of the attack..."
    B. "His case, Korematsu v. The United States..."
    C. "Fred Korematsu was a..."
    D. "This statement effectively pronounced..."

    21.____

22. When put together correctly, the last sentence of the paragraph should end with the words
    A. "...that's what I wanted to do."   B. "...were ordered to leave."
    C. "...during World War II."   D. "...was both swift and harsh."

    22.____

Questions 23-25.

DIRECTIONS: Questions 23 through 25 are to be answered on the basis of the following passage.

Over the past two decades, her personal finances have been eroded by illness, divorce, the cost of raising two children, the housing bust, and the economic downturn. "There are more people attending college, more people taking out loans, and more people taking out a higher dollar amount of loans," says Matthew Ward, associate director of media relations at the New York Fed. Anderson, who is 57, told her complicated story at a recent Senate Aging Committee hearing (she's previously appeared on the CBS Evening News). Some 3 percent of U.S. households that are headed by a senior citizen now hold federal student debt, mostly debt they took on to finance their own educations, according to a new report from the Government Accountability Office (GAO), an independent agency. She hasn't been able to afford payments on her loans for nearly eight years. Rosemary Anderson has a master's degree, a good job at the University of California (Santa Cruz), and student loans that she could be paying off until she's 81. Student debt has risen across every age group over the past decade, according to a Federal Reserve Bank of New York analysis of credit report data... "As the baby boomers continue to move into retirement, the number of older Americans with defaulted loans will only continue to increase," the report warned. She first enrolled in college in her thirties.

23. When organized correctly, the first sentence should begin with the words
 A. "She first enrolled…"
 B. "Anderson, who is 57…"
 C. "Some 3 percent of…"
 D. "Rosemary Anderson has…"

24. If the author wished to split the paragraph into two paragraphs (not necessarily equal in length), the first sentence of the second paragraph would begin with the words
 A. "Some 3 percent of…"
 B. "There are more people…"
 C. "Over the past two decades…"
 D. "She first enrolled…"

25. When put in the correct order, the second to last sentence should end with the words
 A. "…an independent agency."
 B. "…of credit report data."
 C. "…at the New York Fed."
 D. "…in her thirties."

KEY (CORRECT ANSWERS)

1.	A		11.	A
2.	C		12.	B
3.	B		13.	C
4.	D		14.	A
5.	D		15.	C
6.	B		16.	D
7.	C		17.	A
8.	A		18.	D
9.	C		19.	B
10.	D		20.	C

21. C
22. B
23. D
24. A
25. B

TEST 2

DIRECTIONS: The sentences listed below are part of a meaningful paragraph, but they are not given in their proper order. You are to decide what would be the BEST order to put sentences to form a well-organized paragraph. Each sentence has a place in the paragraph; there are no extra sentences. *PRINT THE LETTER OF THE CORRECT ANSWER IN THE SPACE AT THE RIGHT.*

Questions 1-3.

DIRECTIONS: Questions 1 through 3 are to be answered on the basis of the following passage.

According to the World Health Organization (WHO), exposure to ambient (outdoor) air pollution causes 3 million premature deaths around the world each year, largely due to heart and lung diseases. Air pollution also contributes to such environmental threats as smog, acid rain, depletion of the ozone layer, and global climate change. The U.S. Environmental Protection Agency (EPA) sets National Ambient Air Quality Standards (NAAQS) for those four pollutants as well as carbon monoxide (CO) and lead. The EPA also regulates 187 toxic air pollutants, such as asbestos, benzene, dioxin, and mercury. Finally, the EPA places limits on emissions of greenhouse gases like carbon dioxide (CO_2) and methane, which contribute to global climate change. The WHO has established Air Quality Guidelines (ACGs) to identify safe levels of exposure to the emission of four harmful air pollutants worldwide: particulate matter (PM), ozone (O_3), nitrogen dioxide (NO_2), and sulfur dioxide (SO_2). Since EPA criteria define the allowable concentrations of these six substances in ambient air throughout the United States, they are known as criteria air pollutants. Air pollution refers to the release into the air of chemicals and other substances, known as pollutants, that are potentially harmful to human health and the environment.

1. When organized correctly, the first sentence of this paragraph should begin　　　　1.____
   A. "Air pollution refers…"
   B. "The EPA also regulates..,"
   C. "The WHO has established…"
   D. "According to the…"

2. When put in the correct order, the fourth sentence should end with the words　　　　2.____
   A. "…to global climate change."
   B. "…as criteria air pollutants."
   C. "…nitrogen dioxide (NO_2), and sulfur dioxide (SO_2)."
   D. "…health and the environment."

3. If put in the most logical order, the paragraph would end with the words　　　　3.____
   A. "…as criteria air pollutants."
   B. "…to global climate change."
   C. "…benzene, dioxin, and mercury."
   D. "…human health and the environment."

Questions 4-6.

DIRECTIONS: Questions 4 through 6 are to be answered on the basis of the following passage.

Although gentrification has been associated with some positive impacts, such as urban revitalization and lower crime rates, critics charge that it marginalizes racial and ethnic minorities and destroys the character of urban neighborhoods. British sociologist Ruth Glass is credited with coining the term "gentrification" in her 1964 book *London: Aspects of Change*, which described the transformation that occurred when members of the gentry (an elite or privileged social class) took over working-class districts of London. Gentrification is a type of neighborhood change, a broader term that encompasses various physical, demographic, social, and economic processes that affect distinct residential areas. The arrival of wealthier people leads to new economic development and an increase in property values and rent, which often makes housing unaffordable for longtime residents. Gentrification is a transformation process that typically occurs in urban neighborhoods when higher-income people move in and displace lower-income existing residents.

4. When organized in the correct order, the first sentence of the paragraph should begin with the words
   A. "Gentrification is a type of…"
   B. "British sociologist Ruth…"
   C. "The arrival of…"
   D. "Gentrification is a transformation…"

4._____

5. If put together in the correct order, the second to last sentence in the paragraph would end with the words
   A. "…lower-income existing residents."
   B. "…that affect distinct residential areas."
   C. "…character of urban neighborhoods."
   D. "…working-class districts of London."

5._____

6. If the author wished to change the beginning of the final sentence to "in the end." to better signal the finish of the paragraph, which of the following words would the phrase appear in front of?
   A. British
   B. Gentrification
   C. Although
   D. The

6._____

Questions 7-11.

DIRECTIONS: Questions 7 through 11 are to be answered on the basis of the following passage.

The primary signs of ADHD include a persistent pattern of inattention or hyperactivity lasting in duration for six months or longer with an onset before 12 years of age. Children with ADHD often experience peer rejection, neglect, or teasing and family interactions may contain high levels of discord and negative interactions (APA, 2013). Two primary types of the disorder include inattentive and hyperactive/impulsive, with a combined type when both inattention and hyperactivity occur together. Inattentive ADHD is evidenced by executive functioning deficits such as being off task, lacking sustained focus, and being disorganized. Hyperactive ADHD is evidenced by excessive talkativeness and fidgeting, with an inability to control impulses that may result in harm. Attention Deficit Hyperactivity Disorder (ADHD) is a commonly diagnosed childhood behavioral disorder affecting millions of children in the U.S. every year (National Institute of Mental Health [NIMH], 2012), with prevalence rates between 5% and 11% of the population. Other research has examined singular traits such as executive function deficits in the school setting, task performance in the school setting (Berk, 1986), driving and awareness of time. However, researching academic aspects of the school experience does not provide a comprehensive understanding of the systemic effects of ADHD in the school environment. Historically, much research on ADHD has focused on the academic impact of behavioral symptoms such as reading and mathematics. These behaviors are inappropriate for the child's age level and symptoms typically interfere with functioning in multiple environments.

7. If the author put the paragraph into a logical order, the first sentence would begin with the words
   A. "Inattentive ADHD is..."
   B. "Historically, much research..."
   C. "These behaviors are..."
   D. "Attention Deficit Hyperactivity Disorder..."

7.____

8. When put in the correct order, what does the author mean by "These behaviors" in the sentence that begins "These behaviors are..."?
   A. Inattention or hyperactivity
   B. Reading and Mathematics
   C. Peer rejection
   D. Sustained focus

8.____

9. If the author wished to split this paragraph into two paragraphs (not necessarily equal parts), the first sentence of the second paragraph would BEGIN with the words
   A. "Historically, much research..."
   B. "Other research has examined..."
   C. "Two primary types of..."
   D. "Inattentive ADHD is evidenced..."

9.____

10. When put in the correct order, the third sentence in the paragraph would END with the words
    A. "...an onset before 12 years of age."
    B. "...5% and 11% of the population."
    C. "...such as reading and mathematics."
    D. "...in multiple environments."

10.____

11. If the above paragraph was organized correctly, its ending words of the last sentence would be
    A. "...sustained focus, and being disorganized."
    B. "...an onset before 12 years of age."
    C. "...in the school environment."
    D. "...inattention and hyperactivity occur together."

11.____

Questions 12-15.

DIRECTIONS: Questions 12 through 15 are to be answered on the basis of the following passage.

Health care fraud imposes huge costs on society. In prosecutions of fraud, the DOJ employs the resources of its own criminal and civil divisions, as well as those of the U.S. Attorneys' Offices, HHS, and the FBI. The FBI estimates that health care fraud accounts for at least three and possibly up to ten percent of total health care expenditures, or somewhere between $82 billion and $272 billion each year. Providers are also careful to screen hires for excluded persons or entities lest they be subject to civil monetary penalties. Several government agencies are involved in fighting health care fraud. Individual states assist the HHS Office of the Inspector General ("OIG") and Centers for Medicare & Medicaid Services ("CMS") to initiate and pursue investigations of Medicare and Medicaid fraud. In addition, the OIG uses its permissive exclusion authority to exclude individuals and entities convicted of health care related crimes from federally funded health care services in order to induce providers to help track fraud through a voluntary disclosure program. $30 to $98 billion dollars of that (approximately 36%) is fraud against the public health programs Medicare and Medicaid. The Department of Justice ("DOJ") and the Department of Health and Human Services ("HHS") enforce federal health care fraud law and regulations.

12. When put together in a logical order, the second sentence of the paragraph would end with the words
    A. "...in fighting health care fraud."
    B. "...$272 billion each year."
    C. "...voluntary disclosure program."
    D. "...to civil monetary penalties."

13. In order to organize the paragraph correctly, the sentence that begins "In addition, the OIG..." should FOLLOW the sentence that begins with the words
    A. "$30 to $98 billion dollars of that..."
    B. "Health care fraud..."
    C. "Individual states assist..."
    D. "In prosecutions of fraud..."

14. The author wishes to split the paragraph into a smaller introductory paragraph followed by a slightly longer body paragraph. Which of the following sentences would be BEST to start the second paragraph?
    A. "$30 to $98 billion dollars of that (approximately 36%) is fraud against the public health care programs Medicare and Medicaid."
    B. "Several government agencies are involved in fighting health care fraud."
    C. "In prosecutions of fraud, the DOJ employs the resources of its own criminal and civil divisions, as well as those of the U.S. Attorneys' Offices, HHS, and the FBI."
    D. "Health care fraud imposes huge costs on society."

15. If put together correctly, the paragraph should end with the words   15.____
    A. "...Attorneys' Offices, HHS, and the FBI."
    B. "...huge costs on society."
    C. "...fighting health care fraud."
    D. "...of Medicare and Medicaid fraud."

Questions 16-19.

DIRECTIONS: Questions 16 through 19 are to be answered on the basis of the following passage.

President Abraham Lincoln advocated for granting amnesty to former Confederates to heal the country after the devastating war. Adams and his fellow Federalist Party members in Congress used the law to jail more than a dozen of his political rivals. In 1977, President Jimmy Carter lifted the restrictions on draft dodgers, granting them unconditional amnesty. The issue of amnesty again arose shortly after the U.S. Civil War (1861-1865). Some U.S. government officials, including Vice President Andrew Johnson, advocating placing severe punishments on the military and civilian leaders of the secessionist Confederate States of America. A century later, the controversial nature of the Vietnam War (1964-1975), combined with the compulsory draft for military service, compelled many young men of eligible age to violate the law to avoid the draft. When Thomas Jefferson, Adams' Vice President and opponent of the Alien and Sedition Acts, won the 1800 presidential election, he declared amnesty for those found to have violated the law. Other young men who were drafted deserted the army and refused to serve. In May 1865, when serving as president following Lincoln's assassination, Johnson issued the Proclamation of Amnesty and Reconstruction, which granted the rights of voting and holding office to most former Confederates. In 1974, President Gerald Ford granted amnesty to deserters and "draft dodgers" on the condition that they swear allegiance to the United States and engage in two years of community service. In 1798, President John Adams signed the Alien and Sedition Acts, a set of four laws that restricted criticism of the federal government.

16. When put in the correct order, the paragraph would begin with the following words.   16.____
    A. "Some U.S. government..."   B. "In May 1865, when..."
    C. "A century later, the..."   D. "In 1798, President..."

17. If put in logical order, what sentence number would the sentence that begins   17.____
    "President Abraham Lincoln..." be?
    A. One   B. Six   C. Five   D. Two

18. The author wants to split this paragraph into three separate paragraphs. The   18.____
    THIRD paragraph should begin with the words
    A. "The issue of amnesty again..."   B. "In 1798, President..."
    C. "In 1977, President Jimmy..."   D. "A century later, the..."

19. When organized in sequential order, the last sentence of the paragraph   19.____
    would end with the words
    A. "...of his political rivals."   B. "...after the devastating war."
    C. "...them unconditional amnesty."   D. "...of the federal government."

Questions 20-22.

DIRECTIONS: Questions 20 through 22 are to be answered on the basis of the following passage.

Throughout history, militias have played an important role in national defense against foreign invaders or oppressors. In the original American colonies, state militias served to keep order and played an important role in the fight for independence from the British during the American Revolutionary War. Since that time, state-level militias have continued to exist in the United States alongside a national standing army, providing additional reserve defense and emergency assistance when needed. Some countries still rely almost entirely on public militias for civil defense. In Switzerland, for example, all able-bodied males must serve as part of the Swiss military or civilian service for several months starting when they turn 20 years old and remain reserve militia for years after. Similarly, in Israel, all non-Arab citizens over the age of 18 are required to serve in the Israel Defense Forces for at least two years; Israel is unique in that it requires military service from female citizens as well as males.

20. When put into the correct order, the paragraph should begin with the words 20.____
    A. "Throughout history, militias..."   B. "Similarly, in Israel..."
    C. "Some countries still rely..."   D. "Since that time, state-level..."

21. The fifth sentence of the paragraph should end with the words 21.____
    A. "...against foreign invaders or oppressors."
    B. "...militias for civil defense."
    C. "...reserve militia for years after."
    D. "...citizens as well as males."

22. The last sentence of the paragraph should end with the words 22.____
    A. "...militias for civil defense."
    B. "...citizens as well as males."
    C. "...against foreign invaders or oppressors."
    D. "...during the American Revolutionary War."

Questions 23-25.

DIRECTIONS: Questions 23 through 25 are to be answered on the basis of the following passage.

Medicines such as herbal and homeopathic remedies differ radically from those typically prescribed by mainstream physicians. These practices derive from different cultural traditions and scientific premises. As of 2012, the Memorial Sloan-Kettering Cancer Center offered hypnosis and tai chi, which is an ancient Chinese exercise, to help eases the pains associated with conventional cancer treatments. Some medical professionals staunchly dismiss a number of alternative techniques and theories as quackery. The concept of alternative medicine encompasses an extremely wide range of therapeutic modalities, from acupuncture to yoga. As of 2012, nearly 40 percent of Americans use some alternative medicines or therapies, according to the National Institutes of Health's National Center for Complementary and Alternative Medicine. Alternative approaches to health, fitness, disease prevention, and treatment are sometimes referred to as holistic health care or natural medicine. These names suggest some of the philosophical foundations shared by traditions such as homeopathy, naturopathy, traditional Chinese medicine and herbal medicine. A University of Pennsylvania study in 2010 found that more than 70 percent of U.S. cancer centers offered information on complementary therapies. Increasingly, health care providers are encouraging patients to combine alternative and conventional (or allopathic) treatments, a practice known as complementary or integrative medicine. In the contemporary United States, the phrase alternative medicine has come to mean virtually any healing or wellness practice not based within the conventional system of medical doctors, nurses, and hospitals. Some of these alternative treatments include acupuncture to alleviate pain and nausea and yoga to help reduce stress and manage pain. Yet taken as a whole, the alternative sector of the health field is enormously popular and rapidly growing. The Health Services Research Journal reported in 2011 that three out of four U.S. health care workers used complementary or alternative medicine practices themselves. Other studies have shown that more medical professionals are recommending that cancer patients seek alternative treatments to deal with the side effects of conventional treatments, such as chemotherapy, radiation, and surgery.

23. When put in the correct order, the first sentence should begin with the words
    A. "A University of Pennsylvania study…"
    B. "Other studies have shown that…"
    C. "Increasingly, health care providers…"
    D. "In the contemporary United States…"

24. If the author were to split the paragraph into two separate ones, the first sentence of the second paragraph should begin with the words
    A. "Alternative approaches to health…"
    B. "The concept of alternative medicine…"
    C. "As of 2012, nearly 40%..."
    D. "These names suggest some…"

25. When put into the correct logical sequence, the paragraph should end with the words
    A. "…Complementary and Alternative Medicine."
    B. "…system of medical doctors, nurses, and hospitals."
    C. "…associated with conventional cancer treatments."
    D. "…health care or natural medicine."

KEY (CORRECT ANSWERS)

1.	A		11.	C
2.	C		12.	B
3.	B		13.	C
4.	D		14.	B
5.	B		15.	A
6.	C		16.	D
7.	D		17.	B
8.	A		18.	D
9.	A		19.	C
10.	D		20.	A

21. C
22. B
23. D
24. A
25. C

PHILOSOPHY, PRINCIPLES, PRACTICES, AND TECHNICS OF SUPERVISION, ADMINISTRATION, MANAGEMENT, AND ORGANIZATION

TABLE OF CONTENTS

	Page
MEANING OF SUPERVISION	1
THE OLD AND THE NEW SUPERVISION	1
THE EIGHT (8) BASIC PRINCIPLES OF THE NEW SUPERVISION	1
I. Principle of Responsibility	1
II. Principle of Authority	2
III. Principle of Self-Growth	2
IV. Principle of Individual Worth	2
V. Principle of Creative Leadership	2
VI. Principle of Success and Failure	2
VII. Principle of Science	3
VIII. Principle of Cooperation	3
WHAT IS ADMINISTRATION?	3
I. Practices Commonly Classed as "Supervisory"	3
II. Practices Commonly Classed as "Administrative"	3
III. Practices Commonly Classed as Both "Supervisory" and "Administrative"	4
RESPONSIBILITIES OF THE SUPERVISOR	4
COMPETENCIES OF THE SUPERVISOR	4
THE PROFESSIONAL SUPERVISOR-EMPLOYEE RELATIONSHIP	4
MINI-TEXT IN SUPERVISION, ADMINISTRATION, MANAGEMENT, AND ORGANIZATION	5
I. Brief Highlights	5
A. Levels of Management	6
B. What the Supervisor Must Learn	6
C. A Definition of Supervision	6
D. Elements of the Team Concept	6
E. Principles of Organization	6
F. The Four Important Parts of Every Job	7
G. Principles of Delegation	7
H. Principles of Effective Communications	7
I. Principles of Work Improvement	7
J. Areas of Job Improvement	7
K. Seven Key Points in Making Improvements	8

	L.	Corrective Techniques for Job Improvement	8
	M.	A Planning Checklist	8
	N.	Five Characteristics of Good Directions	9
	O.	Types of Directions	9
	P.	Controls	9
	Q.	Orienting the New Employee	9
	R.	Checklist for Orienting New Employees	9
	S.	Principles of Learning	10
	T.	Causes of Poor Performance	10
	U.	Four Major Steps in On-the-Job Instructions	10
	V.	Employees Want Five Things	10
	W.	Some Don'ts in Regard to Praise	11
	X.	How to Gain Your Workers' Confidence	11
	Y.	Sources of Employee Problems	11
	Z.	The Supervisor's Key to Discipline	11
	AA.	Five Important Processes of Management	12
	BB.	When the Supervisor Fails to Plan	12
	CC.	Fourteen General Principles of Management	12
	DD.	Change	12
II.	Brief Topical Summaries		13
	A.	Who/What is the Supervisor?	13
	B.	The Sociology of Work	13
	C.	Principles and Practices of Supervision	14
	D.	Dynamic Leadership	14
	E.	Processes for Solving Problems	15
	F.	Training for Results	15
	G.	Health, Safety, and Accident Prevention	16
	H.	Equal Employment Opportunity	16
	I.	Improving Communications	16
	J.	Self-Development	17
	K.	Teaching and Training	17
		1. The Teaching Process	17
		a. Preparation	17
		b. Presentation	18
		c. Summary	18
		d. Application	18
		e. Evaluation	18
		2. Teaching Methods	18
		a. Lecture	18
		b. Discussion	18
		c. Demonstration	19
		d. Performance	19
		e. Which Method to Use	19

PHILOSOPHY, PRINCIPLES, PRACTICES, AND TECHNICS OF SUPERVISION, ADMINISTRATION, MANAGEMENT, AND ORGANIZATION

MEANING OF SUPERVISION

The extension of the democratic philosophy has been accompanied by an extension in the scope of supervision. Modern leaders and supervisors no longer think of supervision in the narrow sense of being confined chiefly to visiting employees, supplying materials, or rating the staff. They regard supervision as being intimately related to all the concerned agencies of society, they speak of the supervisor's function in terms of "growth," rather than the "improvement" of employees.

This modern concept of supervision may be defined as follows: Supervision is leadership and the development of leadership within groups which are cooperatively engaged in inspection, research, training, guidance, and evaluation.

THE OLD AND THE NEW SUPERVISION

TRADITIONAL
1. Inspection
2. Focused on the employee
3. Visitation
4. Random and haphazard
5. Imposed and authoritarian
6. One person usually

MODERN
1. Study and analysis
2. Focused on aims, materials, methods, supervisors, employees, environment
3. Demonstrations, intervisitation, workshops, directed reading, bulletins, etc.
4. Definitely organized and planned (scientific)
5. Cooperative and democratic
6. Many persons involved (creative)

THE EIGHT (8) BASIC PRINCIPLES OF THE NEW SUPERVISION

I. Principle of Responsibility
   Authority to act and responsibility for acting must be joined.
   A. If you give responsibility, give authority.
   B. Define employee duties clearly.
   C. Protect employees from criticism by others.
   D. Recognize the rights as well as obligations of employees.
   E. Achieve the aims of a democratic society insofar as it is possible within the area of your work.
   F. Establish a situation favorable to training and learning.
   G. Accept ultimate responsibility for everything done in your section, unit, office, division, department.
   H. Good administration and good supervision are inseparable.

II. Principle of Authority
The success of the supervisor is measured by the extent to which the power of authority is not used.
   A. Exercise simplicity and informality in supervision
   B. Use the simplest machinery of supervision
   C. If it is good for the organization as a whole, it is probably justified.
   D. Seldom be arbitrary or authoritative.
   E. Do not base your work on the power of position or of personality.
   F. Permit and encourage the free expression of opinions.

III. Principle of Self-Growth
The success of the supervisor is measured by the extent to which, and the speed with which, he is no longer needed.
   A. Base criticism on principles, not on specifics.
   B. Point out higher activities to employees.
   C. Train for self-thinking by employees to meet new situations.
   D. Stimulate initiative, self-reliance, and individual responsibility
   E. Concentrate on stimulating the growth of employees rather than on removing defects.

IV. Principle of Individual Worth
Respect for the individual is a paramount consideration in supervision.
   A. Be human and sympathetic in dealing with employees.
   B. Don't nag about things to be done.
   C. Recognize the individual differences among employees and seek opportunities to permit best expression of each personality.

V. Principle of Creative Leadership
The best supervision is that which is not apparent to the employee.
   A. Stimulate, don't drive employees to creative action.
   B. Emphasize doing good things.
   C. Encourage employees to do what they do best.
   D. Do not be too greatly concerned with details of subject or method.
   E. Do not be concerned exclusively with immediate problems and activities.
   F. Reveal higher activities and make them both desired and maximally possible.
   G. Determine procedures in the light of each situation but see that these are derived from a sound basic philosophy.
   H. Aid, inspire, and lead so as to liberate the creative spirit latent in all good employees.

VI. Principle of Success and Failure
There are no unsuccessful employees, only unsuccessful supervisors who have failed to give proper leadership.
   A. Adapt suggestions to the capacities, attitudes, and prejudices of employees.
   B. Be gradual, be progressive, be persistent.
   C. Help the employee find the general principle; have the employee apply his own problem to the general principle.
   D. Give adequate appreciation for good work and honest effort.
   E. Anticipate employee difficulties and help to prevent them.
   F. Encourage employees to do the desirable things they will do anyway.
   G. Judge your supervision by the results it secures.

VII. Principle of Science
Successful supervision is scientific, objective, and experimental. It is based on facts, not on prejudices.
    A. Be cumulative in results.
    B. Never divorce your suggestions from the goals of training.
    C. Don't be impatient of results.
    D. Keep all matters on a professional, not a personal, level.
    E. Do not be concerned exclusively with immediate problems and activities.
    F. Use objective means of determining achievement and rating where possible.

VIII. Principle of Cooperation
Supervision is a cooperative enterprise between supervisor and employee.
    A. Begin with conditions as they are.
    B. Ask opinions of all involved when formulating policies.
    C. Organization is as good as its weakest link.
    D. Let employees help to determine policies and department programs.
    E. Be approachable and accessible—physically and mentally.
    F. Develop pleasant social relationships.

WHAT IS ADMINISTRATION

Administration is concerned with providing the environment, the material facilities, and the operational procedures that will promote the maximum growth and development of supervisors and employees. (Organization is an aspect and a concomitant of administration.)

There is no sharp line of demarcation between supervision and administration; these functions are intimately interrelated and, often, overlapping. They are complementary activities.

I. Practices Commonly Classed as "Supervisory"
    A. Conducting employees' conferences
    B. Visiting sections, units, offices, divisions, departments
    C. Arranging for demonstrations
    D. Examining plans
    E. Suggesting professional reading
    F. Interpreting bulletins
    G. Recommending in-service training courses
    H. Encouraging experimentation
    I. Appraising employee morale
    J. Providing for intervisitation

II. Practices Commonly Classified as "Administrative"
    A. Management of the office
    B. Arrangement of schedules for extra duties
    C. Assignment of rooms or areas
    D. Distribution of supplies
    E. Keeping records and reports
    F. Care of audio-visual materials
    G. Keeping inventory records
    H. Checking record cards and books

     I.   Programming special activities
     J.   Checking on the attendance and punctuality of employees

III. Practices Commonly Classified as Both "Supervisory" and "Administrative"
    A. Program construction
    B. Testing or evaluating outcomes
    C. Personnel accounting
    D. Ordering instructional materials

RESPONSIBILITIES OF THE SUPERVISOR

A person employed in a supervisory capacity must constantly be able to improve his own efficiency and ability. He represent the employer to the employees and only continuous self-examination can make him a capable supervisor.

Leadership and training are the supervisor's responsibility. An efficient working unit is one in which the employees work with the supervisor. It is his job to bring out the best in his employees. He must always be relaxed, courteous, and calm in his association with his employees. Their feelings are important, and a harsh attitude does not develop the most efficient employees.

COMPETENCES OF THE SUPERVISOR

    I.   Complete knowledge of the duties and responsibilities of his position.
    II.   To be able to organize a job, plan ahead, and carry through.
    III. To have self-confidence and initiative.
    IV. To be able to handle the unexpected situation and make quick decisions.
    V.   To be able to properly train subordinates in the positions they are best suited for.
    VI. To be able to keep good human relations among his subordinates.
    VII. To be able to keep good human relations between his subordinates and himself and to earn their respect and trust.

THE PROFESSIONAL SUPERVISOR-EMPLOYEE RELATIONSHIP

There are two kinds of efficiency: one kind is only apparent and is produced in organizations through the exercise of mere discipline; this is but a simulation of the second, or true, efficiency which springs from spontaneous cooperation. If you are a manager, no matter how great or small your responsibility, it is your job, in the final analysis, to create and develop this involuntary cooperation among the people whom you supervise. For, no matter how powerful a combination of money, machines, and materials a company may have, this is a dead and sterile thing without a team of willing, thinking, and articulate people to guide it.

The following 21 points are presented as indicative of the exemplary basic relationship that should exist between supervisor and employee:

1. Each person wants to be liked and respected by his fellow employee and wants to be treated with consideration and respect by his superior.
2. The most competent employee will make an error. However, in a unit where good relations exist between the supervisor and his employees, tenseness and fear do not exist. Thus, errors are not hidden or covered up, and the efficiency of a unit is not impaired.

3. Subordinates resent rules, regulations, or orders that are unreasonable or unexplained.
4. Subordinates are quick to resent unfairness, harshness, injustices, and favoritism.
5. An employee will accept responsibility if he knows that he will be complimented for a job well done, and not too harshly chastised for failure; that his supervisor will check the cause of the failure, and, if it was the supervisor's fault, he will assume the blame therefore. If it was the employee's fault, his supervisor will explain the correct method or means of handling the responsibility.
6. An employee wants to receive credit for a suggestion he has made, that is used. If a suggestion cannot be used, the employee is entitled to an explanation. The supervisor should not say "no" and close the subject.
7. Fear and worry slow up a worker's ability. Poor working environment can impair his physical and mental health. A good supervisor avoids forceful methods, threats, and arguments to get a job done.
8. A forceful supervisor is able to train his employees individually and as a team, and is able to motivate them in the proper channels.
9. A mature supervisor is able to properly evaluate his subordinates and to keep them happy and satisfied.
10. A sensitive supervisor will never patronize his subordinates.
11. A worthy supervisor will respect his employees' confidences.
12. Definite and clear-cut responsibilities should be assigned to each executive.
13. Responsibility should always be coupled with corresponding authority.
14. No change should be made in the scope or responsibilities of a position without a definite understanding to that effect on the part of all persons concerned.
15. No executive or employee, occupying a single position in the organization, should be subject to definite orders from more than one source.
16. Orders should never be given to subordinates over the head of a responsible executive. Rather than do this, the officer in question should be supplanted.
17. Criticisms of subordinates should, whoever possible, be made privately, and in no case should a subordinate be criticized in the presence of executives or employees of equal or lower rank.
18. No dispute or difference between executives or employees as to authority or responsibilities should be considered too trivial for prompt and careful adjudication.
19. Promotions, wage changes, and disciplinary action should always be approved by the executive immediately superior to the one directly responsible.
20. No executive or employee should ever be required, or expected, to be at the same time an assistant to, and critic of, another.
21. Any executive whose work is subject to regular inspection should, wherever practicable, be given the assistance and facilities necessary to enable him to maintain an independent check of the quality of his work.

MINI-TEXT IN SUPERVISION, ADMINISTRATION, MANAGEMENT, AND ORGANIZATION

I. Brief Highlights

Listed concisely and sequentially are major headings and important data in the field for quick recall and review.

A. Levels of Management
Any organization of some size has several levels of management. In terms of a ladder, the levels are:

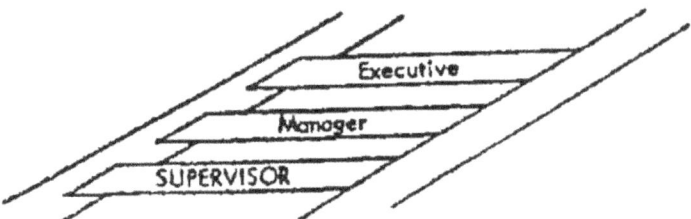

The first level is very important because it is the beginning point of management leadership.

B. What the Supervisor Must Learn
A supervisor must learn to:
1. Deal with people and their differences
2. Get the job done through people
3. Recognize the problems when they exist
4. Overcome obstacles to good performance
5. Evaluate the performance of people
6. Check his own performance in terms of accomplishment

C. A Definition of Supervisor
The term supervisor means any individual having authority, in the interests of the employer, to hire, transfer, suspend, lay-off, recall, promote, discharge, assign, reward, or discipline other employees or responsibility to direct them, or to adjust their grievances, or effectively to recommend such action, if, in connection with the foregoing, exercise of such authority is not of a merely routine or clerical nature but requires the use of independent judgment.

D. Elements of the Team Concept
What is involved in teamwork? The component parts are:
1. Members
2. A leader
3. Goals
4. Plans
5. Cooperation
6. Spirit

E. Principles of Organization
1. A team member must know what his job is.
2. Be sure that the nature and scope of a job are understood.
3. Authority and responsibility should be carefully spelled out.
4. A supervisor should be permitted to make the maximum number of decisions affecting his employees.
5. Employees should report to only one supervisor.
6. A supervisor should direct only as many employees as he can handle effectively.
7. An organization plan should be flexible.

8. Inspection and performance of work should be separate.
9. Organizational problems should receive immediate attention.
10. Assign work in line with ability and experience.

F. The Four Important Parts of Every Job
1. Inherent in every job is the *accountability* for results.
2. A second set of factors in every job is *responsibilities*.
3. Along with duties and responsibilities one must have the *authority* to act within certain limits without obtaining permission to proceed.
4. No job exists in a vacuum. The supervisor is surrounded by key *relationships*.

G. Principles of Delegation
Where work is delegated for the first time, the supervisor should think in terms of these questions:
1. Who is best qualified to do this?
2. Can an employee improve his abilities by doing this?
3. How long should an employee spend on this?
4. Are there any special problems for which he will need guidance?
5. How broad a delegation can I make?

H. Principles of Effective Communications
1. Determine the media.
2. To whom directed?
3. Identification and source authority.
4. Is communication understood?

I. Principles of Work Improvement
1. Most people usually do only the work which is assigned to them.
2. Workers are likely to fit assigned work into the time available to perform it.
3. A good workload usually stimulates output.
4. People usually do their best work when they know that results will be reviewed or inspected.
5. Employees usually feel that someone else is responsible for conditions of work, workplace layout, job methods, type of tools/equipment, and other such factors.
6. Employees are usually defensive about their job security.
7. Employees have natural resistance to change.
8. Employees can support or destroy a supervisor.
9. A supervisor usually earns the respect of his people through his personal example of diligence and efficiency.

J. Areas of Job Improvement
The areas of job improvement are quite numerous, but the most common ones which a supervisor can identify and utilize are:
1. Departmental layout
2. Flow of work
3. Workplace layout
4. Utilization of manpower
5. Work methods
6. Materials handling

7. Utilization
8. Motion economy

K. Seven Key Points in Making Improvements
 1. Select the job to be improved
 2. Study how it is being done now
 3. Question the present method
 4. Determine actions to be taken
 5. Chart proposed method
 6. Get approval and apply
 7. Solicit worker participation

L. Corrective Techniques of Job Improvement
 Specific Problems
 1. Size of workload
 2. Inability to meet schedules
 3. Strain and fatigue
 4. Improper use of men and skills
 5. Waste, poor quality, unsafe conditions
 6. Bottleneck conditions that hinder output
 7. Poor utilization of equipment and machine
 8. Efficiency and productivity of labor

 General Improvement
 1. Departmental layout
 2. Flow of work
 3. Work plan layout
 4. Utilization of manpower
 5. Work methods
 6. Materials handling
 7. Utilization of equipment
 8. Motion economy

 Corrective Techniques
 1. Study with scale model
 2. Flow chart study
 3. Motion analysis
 4. Comparison of units produced to standard allowance
 5. Methods analysis
 6. Flow chart and equipment study
 7. Down time vs. running time
 8. Motion analysis

M. A Planning Checklist
 1. Objectives
 2. Controls
 3. Delegations
 4. Communications
 5. Resources
 6. Manpower

7. Equipment
8. Supplies and materials
9. Utilization of time
10. Safety
11. Money
12. Work
13. Timing of improvements

N. Five Characteristics of Good Directions
In order to get results, directions must be:
1. Possible of accomplishment
2. Agreeable with worker interests
3. Related to mission
4. Planned and complete
5. Unmistakably clear

O. Types of Directions
1. Demands or direct orders
2. Requests
3. Suggestion or implication
4. volunteering

P. Controls
A typical listing of the overall areas in which the supervisor should establish controls might be:
1. Manpower
2. Materials
3. Quality of work
4. Quantity of work
5. Time
6. Space
7. Money
8. Methods

Q. Orienting the New Employee
1. Prepare for him
2. Welcome the new employee
3. Orientation for the job
4. Follow-up

R. Checklist for Orienting New Employees   Yes   No
1. Do you appreciate the feelings of new employees
   when they first report for work?   ___   ___
2. Are you aware of the fact that the new employee must
   make a big adjustment to his job?   ___   ___
3. Have you given him good reasons for liking the job and
   the organization?   ___   ___
4. Have you prepared for his first day on the job?   ___   ___
5. Did you welcome him cordially and make him feel needed?   ___   ___

		Yes	No
6.	Did you establish rapport with him so that he feels free to talk and discuss matters with you?	___	___
7.	Did you explain his job to him and his relationship to you?	___	___
8.	Does he know that his work will be evaluated periodically on a basis that is fair and objective?	___	___
9.	Did you introduce him to his fellow workers in such a way that they are likely to accept him?	___	___
10.	Does he know what employee benefits he will receive?	___	___
11.	Does he understand the importance of being on the job and what to do if he must leave his duty station?	___	___
12.	Has he been impressed with the importance of accident prevention and safe practice?	___	___
13.	Does he generally know his way around the department?	___	___
14.	Is he under the guidance of a sponsor who will teach the right way of doing things?	___	___
15.	Do you plan to follow-up so that he will continue to adjust successfully to his job?	___	___

S. Principles of Learning
1. Motivation
2. Demonstration or explanation
3. Practice

T. Causes of Poor Performance
1. Improper training for job
2. Wrong tools
3. Inadequate directions
4. Lack of supervisory follow-up
5. Poor communications
6. Lack of standards of performance
7. Wrong work habits
8. Low morale
9. Other

U. Four Major Steps in On-The-Job Instruction
1. Prepare the worker
2. Present the operation
3. Tryout performance
4. Follow-up

V. Employees Want Five Things
1. Security
2. Opportunity
3. Recognition
4. Inclusion
5. Expression

W. Some Don'ts in Regard to Praise
1. Don't praise a person for something he hasn't done.
2. Don't praise a person unless you can be sincere.
3. Don't be sparing in praise just because your superior withholds it from you.
4. Don't let too much time elapse between good performance and recognition of it

X. How to Gain Your Workers' Confidence
Methods of developing confidence include such things as:
1. Knowing the interests, habits, hobbies of employees
2. Admitting your own inadequacies
3. Sharing and telling of confidence in others
4. Supporting people when they are in trouble
5. Delegating matters that can be well handled
6. Being frank and straightforward about problems and working conditions
7. Encouraging others to bring their problems to you
8. Taking action on problems which impede worker progress

Y. Sources of Employee Problems
On-the-job causes might be such things as:
1. A feeling that favoritism is exercised in assignments
2. Assignment of overtime
3. An undue amount of supervision
4. Changing methods or systems
5. Stealing of ideas or trade secrets
6. Lack of interest in job
7. Threat of reduction in force
8. Ignorance or lack of communications
9. Poor equipment
10. Lack of knowing how supervisor feels toward employee
11. Shift assignments

Off-the-job problems might have to do with:
1. Health
2. Finances
3. Housing
4. Family

Z. The Supervisor's Key to Discipline
There are several key points about discipline which the supervisor should keep in mind:
1. Job discipline is one of the disciplines of life and is directed by the supervisor.
2. It is more important to correct an employee fault than to fix blame for it.
3. Employee performance is affected by problems both on the job and off.
4. Sudden or abrupt changes in behavior can be indications of important employee problems.
5. Problems should be dealt with as soon as possible after they are identified.
6. The attitude of the supervisor may have more to do with solving problems than the techniques of problem solving.
7. Correction of employee behavior should be resorted to only after the supervisor is sure that training or counseling will not be helpful.

8. Be sure to document your disciplinary actions.
9. Make sure that you are disciplining on the basis of facts rather than personal feelings.
10. Take each disciplinary step in order, being careful not to make snap judgments, or decisions based on impatience.

AA. Five Important Processes of Management
1. Planning
2. Organizing
3. Scheduling
4. Controlling
5. Motivating

BB. When the Supervisor Fails to Plan
1. Supervisor creates impression of not knowing his job
2. May lead to excessive overtime
3. Job runs itself—supervisor lacks control
4. Deadlines and appointments missed
5. Parts of the work go undone
6. Work interrupted by emergencies
7. Sets a bad example
8. Uneven workload creates peaks and valleys
9. Too much time on minor details at expense of more important tasks

CC. Fourteen General Principles of Management
1. Division of work
2. Authority and responsibility
3. Discipline
4. Unity of command
5. Unity of direction
6. Subordination of individual interest to general interest
7. Remuneration of personnel
8. Centralization
9. Scalar chain
10. Order
11. Equity
12. Stability of tenure of personnel
13. Initiative
14. Esprit de corps

DD. Change

Bringing about change is perhaps attempted more often, and yet less well understood, than anything else the supervisor does. How do people generally react to change? (People tend to resist change that is imposed upon them by other individuals or circumstances.

Change is characteristic of every situation. It is a part of every real endeavor where the efforts of people are concerned.

1. Why do people resist change?
   People may resist change because of:
   a. Fear of the unknown
   b. Implied criticism
   c. Unpleasant experiences in the past
   d. Fear of loss of status
   e. Threat to the ego
   f. Fear of loss of economic stability

2. How can we best overcome the resistance to change?
   In initiating change, take these steps:
   a. Get ready to sell
   b. Identify sources of help
   c. Anticipate objections
   d. Sell benefits
   e. Listen in depth
   f. Follow up

II. Brief Topical Summaries

   A. Who/What is the Supervisor?
      1. The supervisor is often called the "highest level employee and the lowest level manager."
      2. A supervisor is a member of both management and the work group. He acts as a bridge between the two.
      3. Most problems in supervision are in the area of human relations, or people problems.
      4. Employees expect: Respect, opportunity to learn and to advance, and a sense of belonging, and so forth.
      5. Supervisors are responsible for directing people and organizing work. Planning is of paramount importance.
      6. A position description is a set of duties and responsibilities inherent to a given position.
      7. It is important to keep the position description up-to-date and to provide each employee with his own copy.

   B. The Sociology of Work
      1. People are alike in many ways; however, each individual is unique.
      2. The supervisor is challenged in getting to know employee differences. Acquiring skills in evaluating individuals is an asset.
      3. Maintaining meaningful working relationships in the organization is of great importance.
      4. The supervisor has an obligation to help individuals to develop to their fullest potential.
      5. Job rotation on a planned basis helps to build versatility and to maintain interest and enthusiasm in work groups.
      6. Cross training (job rotation) provides backup skills.

14

7. The supervisor can help reduce tension by maintaining a sense of humor, providing guidance to employees, and by making reasonable and timely decisions. Employees respond favorably to working under reasonably predictable circumstances.
8. Change is characteristic of all managerial behavior. The supervisor must adjust to changes in procedures, new methods, technological changes, and to a number of new and sometimes challenging situations.
9. To overcome the natural tendency for people to resist change, the supervisor should become more skillful in initiating change.

C. Principles and Practices of Supervision
1. Employees should be required to answer to only one superior.
2. A supervisor can effectively direct only a limited number of employees, depending upon the complexity, variety, and proximity of the jobs involved.
3. The organizational chart presents the organization in graphic form. It reflects lines of authority and responsibility as well as interrelationships of units within the organization.
4. Distribution of work can be improved through an analysis using the "Work Distribution Chart."
5. The "Work Distribution Chart" reflects the division of work within a unit in understandable form.
6. When related tasks are given to an employee, he has a better chance of increasing his skills through training.
7. The individual who is given the responsibility for tasks must also be given the appropriate authority to insure adequate results.
8. The supervisor should delegate repetitive, routine work. Preparation of recurring reports, maintaining leave and attendance records are some examples.
9. Good discipline is essential to good task performance. Discipline is reflected in the actions of employees on the job in the absence of supervision.
10. Disciplinary action may have to be taken when the positive aspects of discipline have failed. Reprimand, warning, and suspension are examples of disciplinary action.
11. If a situation calls for a reprimand, be sure it is deserved and remember it is to be done in private.

D. Dynamic Leadership
1. A style is a personal method or manner of exerting influence.
2. Authoritarian leaders often see themselves as the source of power and authority.
3. The democratic leader often perceives the group as the source of authority and power.
4. Supervisors tend to do better when using the pattern of leadership that is most natural for them.
5. Social scientists suggest that the effective supervisor use the leadership style that best fits the problem or circumstances involved.
6. All four styles—telling, selling, consulting, joining—have their place. Using one does not preclude using the other at another time.

7. The theory X point of view assumes that the average person dislikes work, will avoid it whenever possible, and must be coerced to achieve organizational objectives.
8. The theory Y point of view assumes that the average person considers work to be a natural as play, and, when the individual is committed, he requires little supervision or direction to accomplish desired objectives.
9. The leader's basic assumptions concerning human behavior and human nature affect his actions, decisions, and other managerial practices.
10. Dissatisfaction among employees is often present, but difficult to isolate. The supervisor should seek to weaken dissatisfaction by keeping promises, being sincere and considerate, keeping employees informed, and so forth.
11. Constructive suggestions should be encouraged during the natural progress of the work.

E. Processes for Solving Problems
   1. People find their daily tasks more meaningful and satisfying when they can improve them.
   2. The causes of problems, or the key factors, are often hidden in the background. Ability to solve problems often involves the ability to isolate them from their backgrounds. There is some substance to the cliché that some persons "can't see the forest for the trees."
   3. New procedures are often developed from old ones. Problems should be broken down into manageable parts. New ideas can be adapted from old one.
   4. People think differently in problem-solving situations. Using a logical, patterned approach is often useful. One approach found to be useful includes these steps:
      a. Define the problem
      b. Establish objectives
      c. Get the facts
      d. Weigh and decide
      e. Take action
      f. Evaluate action

F. Training for Results
   1. Participants respond best when they feel training is important to them.
   2. The supervisor has responsibility for the training and development of those who report to him.
   3. When training is delegated to others, great care must be exercised to insure the trainer has knowledge, aptitude, and interest for his work as a trainer.
   4. Training (learning) of some type goes on continually. The most successful supervisor makes certain the learning contributes in a productive manner to operational goals.
   5. New employees are particularly susceptible to training. Older employees facing new job situations require specific training, as well as having need for development and growth opportunities.
   6. Training needs require continuous monitoring.
   7. The training officer of an agency is a professional with a responsibility to assist supervisors in solving training problems.

8. Many of the self-development steps important to the supervisor's own growth are equally important to the development of peers and subordinates. Knowledge of these is important when the supervisor consults with others on development and growth opportunities.

G. Health, Safety, and Accident Prevention
 1. Management-minded supervisors take appropriate measures to assist employees in maintaining health and in assuring safe practices in the work environment.
 2. Effective safety training and practices help to avoid injury and accidents.
 3. Safety should be a management goal. All infractions of safety which are observed should be corrected without exception.
 4. Employees' safety attitude, training and instruction, provision of safe tools and equipment, supervision, and leadership are considered highly important factors which contribute to safety and which can be influenced directly by supervisors.
 5. When accidents do occur, they should be investigated promptly for very important reasons, including the fact that information which is gained can be used to prevent accidents in the future.

H. Equal Employment Opportunity
 1. The supervisor should endeavor to treat all employees fairly, without regard to religion, race, sex, or national origin.
 2. Groups tend to reflect the attitude of the leader. Prejudice can be detected even in very subtle form. Supervisors must strive to create a feeling of mutual respect and confidence in every employee.
 3. Complete utilization of all human resources is a national goal. Equitable consideration should be accorded women in the work force, minority-group members, the physically and mentally handicapped, and the older employee. The important question is: "Who can do the job?"
 4. Training opportunities, recognition for performance, overtime assignments, promotional opportunities, and all other personnel actions are to be handled on an equitable basis.

I. Improving Communications
 1. Communications is achieving understanding between the sender and the receiver of a message. It also means sharing information—the creation of understanding.
 2. Communication is basic to all human activity. Words are means of conveying meanings; however, real meanings are in people.
 3. There are very practical differences in the effectiveness of one-way, impersonal, and two-way communications. Words spoken face-to-face are better understood. Telephone conversations are effective, but lack the rapport of person-to-person exchanges. The whole person communicates.
 4. Cooperation and communication in an organization go hand in hand. When there is a mutual respect between people, spelling out rules and procedures for communicating is unnecessary.
 5. There are several barriers to effective communications. These include failure to listen with respect and understanding, lack of skill in feedback, and misinterpreting the meanings of words used by the speaker. It is also common

practice to listen to what we want to hear, and tune out things we do not want to hear.
6. Communication is management's chief problem. The supervisor should accept the challenge to communicate more effectively and to improve interagency and intra-agency communications.
7. The supervisor may often plan for and conduct meetings. The planning phase is critical and may determine the success or the failure of a meeting.
8. Speaking before groups usually requires extra effort. Stage fright may never disappear completely, but it can be controlled.

J. Self-Development
1. Every employee is responsible for his own self-development.
2. Toastmaster and toastmistress clubs offer opportunities to improve skills in oral communications.
3. Planning for one's own self-development is of vital importance. Supervisors know their own strengths and limitations better than anyone else.
4. Many opportunities are open to aid the supervisor in his developmental efforts, including job assignments; training opportunities, both governmental and non-governmental—to include universities and professional conferences and seminars.
5. Programmed instruction offers a means of studying at one's own rate.
6. Where difficulties may arise from a supervisor's being away from his work for training, he may participate in televised home study or correspondence courses to meet his self-development needs.

K. Teaching and Training
1. The Teaching Process
Teaching is encouraging and guiding the learning activities of students toward established goals. In most cases this process consists of five steps: preparation, presentation, summarization, evaluation, and application.

   a. Preparation
   Preparation is two-fold in nature; that of the supervisor and the employee. Preparation by the supervisor is absolutely essential to success. He must know what, when, where, how, and whom he will teach. Some of the factors that should be considered are:
   1) The objectives
   2) The materials needed
   3) The methods to be used
   4) Employee participation
   5) Employee interest
   6) Training aids
   7) Evaluation
   8) Summarization

   Employee preparation consists in preparing the employee to receive the material. Probably the most important single factor in the preparation of the employee is arousing and maintaining his interest. He must know the objectives of the training, why he is there, how the material can be used, and its importance to him.

b. Presentation
In presentation, have a carefully designed plan and follow it. The plan should be accurate and complete, yet flexible enough to meet situations as they arise. The method of presentation will be determined by the particular situation and objectives.

c. Summary
A summary should be made at the end of every training unit and program. In addition, there may be internal summaries depending on the nature of the material being taught. The important thing is that the trainee must always be able to understand how each part of the new material relates to the whole.

d. Application
The supervisor must arrange work so the employee will be given a chance to apply new knowledge or skills while the material is still clear in his mind and interest is high. The trainee does not really know whether he has learned the material until he has been given a chance to apply it. If the material is not applied, it loses most of its value.

e. Evaluation
The purpose of all training is to promote learning. To determine whether the training has been a success or failure, the supervisor must evaluate this learning.
In the broadest sense, evaluation includes all the devices, methods, skills, and techniques used by the supervisor to keep himself and the employees informed as to their progress toward the objectives they are pursuing. The extent to which the employee has mastered the knowledge, skills, and abilities, or changed his attitudes, as determined by the program objectives, is the extent to which instruction has succeeded or failed.
Evaluation should not be confined to the end of the lesson, day, or program but should be used continuously. We shall note later the way this relates to the rest of the teaching process.

2. Teaching Methods
A teaching method is a pattern of identifiable student and instructor activity used in presenting training material.
All supervisors are faced with the problem of deciding which method should be used at a given time.

a. Lecture
The lecture is direct oral presentation of material by the supervisor. The present trend is to place less emphasis on the trainer's activity and more on that of the trainee.

b. Discussion
Teaching by discussion or conference involves using questions and other techniques to arouse interest and focus attention upon certain areas, and by doing so creating a learning situation. This can be one of the most

valuable methods because it gives the employees an opportunity to express their ideas and pool their knowledge.

    c. Demonstration
The demonstration is used to teach how something works or how to do something. It can be used to show a principle or what the results of a series of actions will be. A well-staged demonstration is particularly effective because it shows proper methods of performance in a realistic manner.

    d. Performance
Performance is one of the most fundamental of all learning techniques or teaching methods. The trainee may be able to tell how a specific operation should be performed but he cannot be sure he knows how to perform the operation until he has done so.
As with all methods, there are certain advantages and disadvantages to each method.

    e. Which Method to Use
Moreover, there are other methods and techniques of teaching. It is difficult to use any method without other methods entering into it. In any learning situation, a combination of methods is usually more effective than any one method alone.

Finally, evaluation must be integrated into the other aspects of the teaching-learning process.

It must be used in the motivation of the trainees; it must be used to assist in developing understanding during the training; and it must be related to employee application of the results of training.

This is distinctly the role of the supervisor.

BASIC FUNDAMENTALS OF OCCUPATIONAL SAFETY AND HEALTH ORGANIZATION

Analysis of safety and health programs in organizations or companies with outstanding records shows that invariably the most successful programs are built around these seven elements:

I. MANAGEMENT LEADERSHIP
   Responsibility
   Policy
II. ASSIGNMENT OF AUTHORITY
   Safety and Health Directors
   Safety and Health Committees
   Small Plant Organizations
   Scattered Operations
III. MAINTENANCE OF SAFE AND HEALTHFUL WORKING CONDITIONS
   Inspection of Work Areas
   Fire Inspections
   Health Surveys
   Job Safety Analysis
IV. ESTABLISHMENT OF SAFETY AND HEALTH TRAINING
   Employee
   Supervisor
   Job Instruction Training
V. ACCIDENT RECORD/DATA COLLECTION SYSTEM
   Records
   Accident Investigation
   Accident Analysis
   Rates
   Countermeasures
VI. HEALTH, MEDICAL AND FIRST AID SYSTEMS
   Health
   Medical
   First Aid
VII. ACCEPTANCE OF PERSONAL ACCOUNTABILITY BY EMPLOYEES
   Maintaining Interest

These seven elements of accident prevention are the same in any industry regardless of the operation and in any establishment or plant, large or small.

I. <u>MANAGEMENT LEADERSHIP</u>

<u>Responsibility</u>

Top management's attitude toward accident prevention in any company or business is almost invariably reflected in the attitude of the supervisory force. Similarly, the employees' attitude is usually the same as the supervisors'. Thus, if the top executive is not genuinely interested in preventing accidents, injuries, and occupational illnesses, no one else is likely to be. Since this basic fact applies to every level of management and supervision, an accident prevention program must have top management's personal commitment and a demonstrated interest if employee cooperation and participation are to be obtained.

Policy

To initiate the program, top management must issue a clear-cut statement of policy for the guidance of middle management, supervisors, and employees. Such a statement of policy will indicate top management's viewpoint in principle, and should cover in general the basic elements.
The details for carrying out an accident prevention program may be assigned, but the responsibility for the basic policy cannot be delegated.
Concern for the safety and health of a firm's employees doesn't stop here but also requires its active interest and participation in all of the major elements of the safety and health organization.

II. ASSIGNMENT OF AUTHORITY

Safety and Health Directors

Safety activities, like any other phase of business, must have leadership and guidance. It is of paramount importance that management assign the authority to direct the safety and health program to one individual. The individual must be formally trained, or the training must be provided on the job in the field of occupational safety and health. The title may be the safety and health director or engineer, the safety manager, or the safety supervisor, depending upon the organization, the nature of the duties assigned, and the personal qualifications. While the occupational safety and health director's exact role varies, the job usually covers:
- Developing and implementing a safety and health program.
- Identifying and controlling hazards.
- Advising management on conformance with company policy and government safety regulations.
- Helping employees understand their safety responsibilities and practices (working through the first line supervisor).
- Evaluating the severity and causes of accidents.
- Evaluating the effectiveness of the safety and health program and improving it where necessary.

To fulfill these responsibilities, persons responsible for safety and health need to maintain direct contact with line and staff supervision.
The first-line supervisor is a key person in the accident prevention program. To the worker, the supervisor is management, because this is the management level that is closest to the people. The supervisor is also the prime communicator with employees on safety and health matters.
With guidance and help from the safety and health director, first-line supervisors should:
Establish safe work practices and conditions.
- Enforce safety rules.
- Teach employees how to recognize hazards.
- Report all injuries and assure prompt treatment.
- Investigate the causes of all accidents and see that action to prevent recurrence is completed.

Accident prevention efforts and results should be included in the supervisor's performance evaluations.

Safety and Health Committees

Safety and health committees are found in almost every successful organization.
In union plants, joint labor-management safety and health committees are established in accordance with the labor agreement.

An efficient, smoothly operating committee is one in which management and employees are in agreement as to the limit of their duties and responsibilities. Also, labor and management <u>must</u> make every effort to carry out their obligations.

The committee organization will vary from plant to plant and from time to time. Much depends upon the size of the organization, the type of problems, and the smoothness and character of employee relations.

The basic function of a safety and health committee is to create and maintain an active interest in safety and health and to reduce accidents and occupational illnesses. The following duties are examples of those sometimes assigned to safety and health committees:

- Make a systematic inspection to discover and report potential health and safety hazards.
- Observe safety practices and procedures of the workforce.
- Review accident reports and corrective measures. Attempt to contribute a positive attitude toward safety and health.
- Listen to employees' concerns about safety and health matters.

Small Plant Organization

Active management and control of the small plant safety and health program may be vested in the chief executive, general manager, or in an experienced and qualified supervisor who has both authority and status.
There are several advantages inherent in small-scale operations, such as closer contact with the working force, more general acquaintance with the problems of the whole plant, and, frequently, less labor turnover. However, it may be difficult to justify a full-time safety and health professional, physician, nurse, or other medical services.

Scattered Operations

Organizations with operations in scattered locations and that require relatively few employees, such as some construction projects, face special inherent problems of organization. Their operations may be seasonal or intermittent and there may not be a sufficiently stable working force to operate committees effectively. The local manager, therefore, needs to adapt the safety and health program to the local conditions.

III. MAINTENANCE OF SAFE AND HEALTHY WORKING CONDITIONS

Inspection of Work Areas

Inspection of work areas can locate hazards and potential hazards which can adversely affect safety and health. Safety inspections are one of the principal means of locating accident sources. Removal of these hazards can lead to substantially improved accident prevention. In promptly correcting work conditions, management demonstrates to the employees its interest and sincerity in accident prevention.

Safety inspections should not be conducted primarily to find how many things are wrong, but rather to determine if everything is satisfactory. The whole purpose should be one of helpfulness in discovering conditions which, if corrected, will bring the plant up to accepted and approved standards.

It is advisable to schedule periodic inspections for the entire facility. Equipment or operations which present the greatest hazards should be inspected more frequently. Such inspections may be made monthly, semi-annually, annually, or at other suitable Intervals. Some types of equipment, such as elevators, boilers, unfired pressure vessels, and fire extinguishing equipment, are required by law to be inspected at specific, regular intervals. Chains, cables, ropes, and other equipment subject to severe strain in handling heavy materials should be inspected at specified intervals. A careful record should be kept of each inspection.

Fire Inspections

One of the hazards having the greatest effect on an industrial plant is fire. Consequently, a system should be set up for periodic inspections of all types of fire protective equipment. Such inspections should include water tanks, sprinkler systems, standpipes, hose, fire plugs, extinguishers, and all other equipment used for fire protection. The schedule of inspections should be closely followed and an accurate record maintained.

Health Surveys

Whenever there is a suspected health hazard, a special inspection should be made to determine the extent of the hazard and the precautions or mechanical safeguarding needed to provide and maintain safe conditions. The services of an industrial hygienist may be needed. Physical examinations should be made of employees exposed to occupational health hazards.

Job Safety Analysis

Job safety analysis (JSA) is a procedure used to review job practices and uncover hazards that may be present. It is one of the first steps in hazard and accident analysis and in safety training. Supervisors and employees in completing the JSA learn more about the job. Study of the JSA will suggest ways for improvement of the job methods, resulting in better work procedures and fewer accidents. A JSA is often kept near a machine so that an operator can review it at any time, especially when starting a new job.

IV. ESTABLISHMENT OF SAFETY AND HEALTH TRAINING

Employees

Effective safety training for all employees is an essential part of any successful accident and illness prevention program. New employees need primary safety orientation to provide a base for future attitude development. They should be taught the specific work practices necessary for their jobs. Job hazards should be identified and proper controls and procedures explained. In beginning on a job, the new employee must be given adequate supervision to assure that the new employee gets started safely.

Supervisors

Supervisors must be trained in all areas of their safety responsibilities, such as hazard identification, job safety analysis, job instruction training, accident investigations, and human relations. Training must be updated whenever processes or operations change. Subjects for training should be related to accident experience.

Job Instruction Training

Job instruction training (JIT), the procedure for teaching a person how to perform a particular job, is accepted as one of the teaching tools in a quality instruction program.

V. ACCIDENT RECORD/DATA COLLECTION SYSTEM

Good recordkeeping is the foundation of a sound approach to occupational safety and health.

Records

Records of accidents and injuries are essential to efficient and successful safety programs, just as records of production, costs, sales, and profits and losses, are essential to the efficient and successful operation of a business. Records supply the information necessary to transform haphazard, costly, ineffective safety work into a planned safety program that controls both conditions and costs.
It is legally required that the company keep proper accident/illness records. It is highly desirable to establish a system for recording all accidents, not just those involving injuries. What may cause a property-damage-only accident today can be the cause of tomorrow's serious-injury accident.
To reduce the possibility of serious complications following a minor accident, there should be a system for reporting all injuries, no matter how trivial, so that prompt first aid treatment can be given and the accident investigated.

Accident Investigation

It is obvious that every accident that occurs should be thoroughly investigated as soon as possible to find its cause and to prevent a recurrence. In addition to accident prevention, other benefits include cost reduction (both the direct and the more sizable indirect costs), continuation of operations or activities without disruption, and the maintenance of good employee morale with its frequently realized higher productivity and fewer work problems.

The important record is the accident investigation report. Every accident should be thoroughly investigated by the immediate supervisor, or depending on its severity, by an accident fact-finding committee appointed by top management.

During the investigation, special inspection of the accident scene is essential. The accident investigation identifies what action should be taken and what improvements are needed to prevent similar accidents occurring in the future. It also documents the facts for use in instances of compensation and litigation.

Accident Analysis

Analyzing accident records will provide convenient and systematized warning. Causal data should be available from the accident report, including such items as the type of injury and body part; general cause, such as unsafe act and/or unsafe conditions; and specific causes such as caught in, contact with, fall from, overexertion, struck by, or struck against. This detail should be analyzed and preventive countermeasures developed.

In the United States, injury and occupational illness records are required by the Occupational Safety and Health Act and specific record requirements are published by OSHA. Injuries and illnesses are recorded separately, with three different categories, as follows:

1. FATALITIES, regardless of the time between the injury and death, or the length of the illness;

2. LOST WORKDAY CASES, other than fatalities, that result in lost workdays;

3. NONFATAL CASES WITHOUT LOST WORKDAYS, which result in transfer to another job or termination of employment, or require medical treatment, or involve loss of consciousness or restriction of work or motion. This category also includes any diagnosed occupational illnesses that are reported to the employer, but are not classified as fatalities or lost workday cases.

Rates

Incidence rates, which relate the total number of injuries and illnesses per category to total employee-hours worked, can be computed from the formula:

$$\frac{\text{Number of injuries and illnesses} \times 200{,}000}{\text{Total hours worked by all employees during the period}}$$

The resulting rate will be expressed as incidents per 100 employees. These rates can be computed by operation within the plant to determine those areas with the most injuries. They can be used to detect incident rate trends within the plant. They can be used to compare your plant with similar plants or your industry.

Countermeasures

Once the accident and/or health hazard(s) has been identified and evaluated, then corrective action must be taken. In general, and in order of effectiveness, the items below should be considered.
- Change the system or machines, method, process, etc., to eliminate the hazard.
- Control the hazard by enclosing, guarding, etc.
- Train employees to increase awareness and to follow
- safe job procedures. Prescribe approved personal protection equipment, etc.

VI. HEALTH, MEDICAL, AND FIRST AID SYSTEMS

Health Services

Occupational health services deal with both the person and the work environment. A comprehensive health program requires (a) concern with all aspects of the work environment that may harm an individual, and (b) a constructive approach to industrial production problems through medical supervision of the employee's health.

The program should be supervised by a physician interested in industrial employees and qualified in industrial medicine. To be effective, the program needs certain medical and first aid facilities, a necessary staff, and the full cooperation of management.

Medical

Preplacement examinations should be conducted to determine and record the physical condition of the prospective worker so that the employee can be assigned to a suitable job. The individual capabilities should meet or exceed the job requirements. Safety must be a factor in the "employee-job fit." Periodic examinations of all employees are sometimes necessary.

First Aid

First aid is an important part of a safety and health program. Immediate, temporary treatment by a qualified individual should be available in the case of accident or sudden illness before the services of a physician can be secured (if they are needed).

VII. ACCEPTANCE OF PERSONAL ACCOUNTABILITY BY EMPLOYEE

Employees make many contributions to the accident prevention programs through the safety suggestions they make and the safety activities in which they participate. But above all, each employee must be trained to work safely and to accept responsibility for his or her own safe work practices. A high degree of employee pride should be developed in the safety record along with the motivation to maintain and improve that record.

To be effective, a program for maintaining interest in safety and health must be based on employee needs. Such activities as contests, drawings, family affairs and award presentations, and the like, serve to reinforce and communicate the safety and health program to the employees. Safety and health programs are a continuing activity, not a one-shot project.

SUMMARY

Successful safety and health programs have distinguishing characteristics. These include:

1. Strong management commitment to safety and health that is shown by various actions reflecting management's support and involvement in activities.
2. Close contact and interaction between workers, supervisors and management enabling open communications on safety and health as well as other job-related matters.
3. Training practices emphasizing early indoctrination and follow-up instruction in job-safety procedures.
4. Evidence of added features of variations in conventional safety and health practices serving to enhance their effectiveness.

www.ingramcontent.com/pod-product-compliance
Lightning Source LLC
Chambersburg PA
CBHW081814300426
44116CB00014B/2362